Powers of Attorney

Trevor M Aldridge
MA (Cantab) Solicitor

Eighth Edition

LAW & TAX

© Longman Group Ltd 1991
© Pearson Professional Limited 1995

Reprinted 1993
Reprinted 1995

Originally written by:
Charles Caplin, LLB, Solicitor

Published by:
Longman Group UK Ltd,
21-27 Lamb's Conduit Street, London WC1 3NJ

Associated offices:
Australia, Hong Kong, Malaysia, Singapore, USA

British Library Cataloguing in Publication Data

Aldridge, Trevor M.
Powers of Attorney.—8th ed.—
(Longman practitioner series)
1. England. Powers of attorney. Law
I. Title
344.206'29

ISBN0-85121-789-3

Printed in Great Britain by The Ipswich Book Company, Suffolk

Contents

Preface to eighth edition

Once again, a new prescribed form of enduring power of attorney—the third—makes a new edition of this book essential. The new form is compulsory for all enduring powers from 31 July 1991, at the end of a year's transitional period when either the second or the third edition of the prescribed form could be used. Unfortunately, the result is even more information which is essential to have to hand, because powers executed earlier, which had to be in the form then current, will continue to be registered and used for many years to come. This book contains the details.

The need for a new edition has afforded the opportunity to take into account other relevant recent changes in the law. An individual no longer executes a deed by sealing it (Law of Property (Miscellaneous Provisions) Act 1989, s 1), and a company does not have to have a common seal nor use it if it does have one (Companies Act 1989, s 130). The Contracts (Applicable Law) Act 1990 will sometimes affect the proper law of powers of attorney, although it has not yet come into force.

The whole text and the precedents have been revised to take into account the changes in the law. I have sought to state the law as it applied on 1 December 1990.

Trevor M Aldridge

Table of Cases

Table of Statutes

Table of Statutory Instruments

Abbreviations

In this book, the following abbreviations are used for the Acts and statutory instruments most commonly referred to:

'1971 Act': Powers of Attorney 1971.

'1985 Act': Enduring Powers of Attorney Act 1985.

'Court Rules': The Court of Protection (Enduring Powers of Attorney) Rules 1986, SI No 127.

'Prescribed Form Regulations': The Enduring Powers of Attorney (Prescribed Form) Regulations 1990, SI No 376.

The 1985 Act followed the recommendations of a Law Commission in its report *The Incapacitated Principal* (Law Com No 122, Cmnd 8977). This is referred to as 'the Law Commission report'.

Chapter 1

Introduction

1 Sources of law

The two statutes that deal in any comprehensive way with powers of attorney are the 1971 Act and the 1985 Act, both of which are reprinted in Appendix 1 (the 1971 Act as since amended). The Trustee Act 1925 (now amended by the 1971 Act) dealt with the grant of powers by trustees, and the relevant section is also reprinted. Other provisions govern the operation of powers of attorney in certain areas of the law.

The statutory provisions are by no means comprehensive, and much of the law in this field is still the common law.

2 Definition: power of attorney

A power of attorney is a document by which one person ('donor') gives another person ('attorney') the power to act on his behalf and in his name. It may be completely general, entitling the attorney to do—almost—everything the donor could himself do, or it may be limited to certain defined objects.

The practical purpose of a power of attorney is not only to invest the attorney with power to act for the donor, but also to provide him with a document defining the extent of his authority, which he can produce as evidence to the third parties with whom he is to deal.

There is no statutory definition of a power of attorney. The 1971 Act provides that 'an instrument creating a power of attorney shall be executed as a deed by the donor of the power' (s 1(1)). This makes it clear that, in general, instruments which are not deeds can no longer validly be powers of attorney as they once could. Formerly, it was only strictly necessary for the power to be granted by deed if authority was required to execute another deed. Nevertheless, the 1971 Act does

1

not invalidate forms of proxy signed by shareholders which, in giving the proxy the power to exercise the shareholder's voting rights, are clearly in the nature of powers of attorney.

3 Enduring powers of attorney

An enduring power of attorney is one which gives an authority which continues even if the donor becomes mentally incapable. Until the 1985 Act came into force on 10 March 1986 (Enduring Powers of Attorney Act 1985 (Commencement) Order 1986), every power was automatically revoked if the donor became mentally incapable. This gave rise to two major inconveniences. First, it was often not clear when the donor became incapable, particularly in the case of a donor gradually failing with the onset of old age. The validity of the power was therefore frequently questionable. Secondly, there was no way in which a person could privately arrange in advance to give someone authority to handle his affairs when, at a later date, he had become incapable. The only mechanism which the law provided was an application by someone else to the Court of Protection to be appointed receiver. That application was made after the patient had become incapable and without his having any say in the selection of the person concerned.

Enduring powers meet both these objections, while introducing safeguards to avoid abuses.

The previous procedures remain unaffected: donors can still grant ordinary powers of attorney, and the Court of Protection can still appoint receivers.

This is, in barest outline, the procedure for creating and using enduring powers of attorney. An enduring power must be granted in a prescribed form which makes it clear to the donor that the power will continue to be effective even if he becomes mentally incapable. The attorney also has to execute it. This achieves two ends. It ensures that the attorney accepts that he should be appointed; an ordinary power can be granted to an attorney who knows nothing of the appointment and is not prepared to accept it. Further, the attorney acknowledges the statutory duty that he may later have to register the power. That duty arises when he has reason to believe that the donor is, or is becoming, mentally incapable. He must then apply to the Court of Protection to register the power, having given notice to the donor of the power and to certain of the donor's relatives.

The powers of an attorney appointed under an enduring power vary, depending on the status of the donor, and the stages in the registration procedure. Until the attorney has reason to believe that the donor is incapable, or is becoming so, he has the full authority conferred by the power. When that time arrives, the attorney's powers are all suspended, but his duty to apply to register arises. Once he has made the application, certain limited authority is automatically restored. When the court registers the enduring power, the attorney can once again exercise all his functions under it.

The Court of Protection has a general jurisdiction over enduring powers of attorney. This includes authorising an attorney to do acts which he would not otherwise be able to do, and revoking the power on exercising its powers under Pt VII of the Mental Health Act 1983 (Management of property and affairs of patients).

4 Authority granted

(a) Ordinary powers of attorney

A normal power of attorney not only delimits the attorney's authority, but it can also specify the way in which he is to exercise his powers. Without more, a power of attorney does not oblige the attorney to take any action, it merely authorises him to do so if he chooses. It has been called a 'one-sided instrument, an instrument which expresses the meaning of the person who makes it, but is not in any sense a contract' (*Chatenay* v *Brazilian Submarine Telegraph Co* [1891] 1 QB 79, 85 per Lindley LJ). This emphasises that the consent of the attorney is not required when a power of attorney is executed in his favour. He has the option not to exercise the authority it confers. An ordinary power of attorney is normally granted by deed poll.

The attorney's position may well change as soon as he takes action pursuant to a power. He then often assumes an obligation, for example, after selling part of the donor's property he may be bound to deposit the proceeds of sale in a particular bank account. This duty is more in the nature of a trust than a contract. The attorney has the discretion of a trustee whether or not to act, but must exercise the discretion in the interest of the donor.

Contractual duties may arise in connection with a power of attorney. The donor normally agrees to ratify the attorney's act under the power, and that is a matter of contract. The power itself may be granted as part of a contract, as in the case of a power incorporated into an equitable mortgage. Also, the attorney may independently have contracted to exercise the powers granted, as in the case of a solicitor who becomes his client's attorney to conclude a transaction in which he has accepted professional instructions.

(b) Enduring powers of attorney

The formalities to create an enduring power of attorney, and the consequences of it, are significantly different from those in respect of an ordinary power. An attorney appointed under an enduring power is a party to it and must execute the instrument (1985 Act, s 2(1)(*b*)). In the absence of special provisions in the enduring power, it does not impose any duty on him, as distinct from giving him authority, to manage the donor's affairs. In this it is the same as an ordinary power. An exception to this general rule may be afforded by the Court of Protection's jurisdiction, once the power has been registered and even before if the court has reason to believe that the donor is becoming or has become mentally incapable (s 5). It can give directions as to the management and disposal by the attorney of the donor's property and affairs, the rendering of accounts and production of records (s 8(2)(*b*)).

The statutory duty which the attorney does undertake by executing the enduring power of attorney is to register the power as soon as he has reason to believe that the donor is becoming, or has become, mentally incapable (s 4(1),(2)). Once that duty has arisen, and until the attorney has made the application to register, his authority is suspended (s 1(1)(*b*)), although the Court of Protection may give him leave to do specified acts (ss 5, 8(2)).

Although an enduring power does not generally oblige the attorney to carry out what it merely authorises him to do, there are special formalities if he wishes to disclaim so that he surrenders his position as attorney. Until the time when he has a duty to register the power, the attorney must give written notice to the donor (s 2(12)), and after that time has arisen, to the court (ss 4(6), 7(1) (*b*)).

5 Power coupled with an interest

A power of attorney may be used as part of a contractual arrangement between the donor and the attorney, to conclude the transaction in the agreed manner, either conditionally or without conditions. The grant of the power by the donor is part of the consideration that he provides in exchange for that provided by the attorney. This contractual arrangement is a power coupled with an interest.

In this case, the interest of the attorney is essentially a proprietary and beneficial one. That has two consequences. First, it will often be part of the bargain that the power of attorney is not revoked for a specified period, or that it is irrevocable. Such a restriction on the donor's normal power of revocation is binding. Secondly, the power is expressly granted to enable the attorney to obtain a benefit for which he has contracted. He therefore exercises the power in his own interest, rather than in the donor's interest.

Examples of powers coupled with an interest are given in Chapter 18 (p 113).

6 Limits on powers of attorney

There are limits on the powers that can be delegated by a power of attorney. The general form of power prescribed by the 1971 Act confers 'authority to do on behalf of the donor anything which he can lawfully do by an attorney' (s 10(1)). This formula is also used by the 1985 Act (s 3(2)). Neither statute defines those limits.

Some restrictions on delegation stem from the donor's position, others from the nature of the action to be performed. There may also be practical limitations. It seems unlikely, for example, that a life assurance company would accept a proposal and medical history form signed by an attorney, even though the prospective assured could validly authorise the attorney to complete it.

(a) Agents

The maxim *delegatus not potest delegare* means that an attorney cannot further delegate his authority, by appointing an attorney to carry out those functions in his stead, unless the terms of the appointment permit it. An enduring power of attorney cannot give the attorney the right to appoint a substitute or successor (1985 Act, s 2(9)). There is however, a limited statutory exception to this rule (Trustee Act 1925, s 25(6); p 27).

(b) Appointments

Those who have appointments of a personal nature cannot delegate their functions to an attorney. This applies, eg, to a director of a company, although the articles of association of some companies expressly allow directors to appoint alternate directors (eg, Table A, arts 65–69: Companies (Tables A to F) Regulations 1985). It also applies to those elected or appointed to public office, and to those employed whether under a contract of service or a contract for services.

(c) Statutory authority

Statutory authority granted to a particular person cannot be delegated. This applies, for example, to the right to practise as a

doctor or a solicitor on duly qualifying, and to the rights conferred on
the grant of a licence. However, a distinction must be drawn between
a licensee's privileges and administrative collateral matters. A person
licensed to sell alcoholic liquor cannot appoint an attorney to sell
drink on his behalf. Yet it is common in the tenancy agreements of
public houses for the tenant to appoint the landlord or his nominee as
attorney to concur in the transfer of the licence when the tenancy
comes to an end.

(d) Wills

A will must be 'signed . . . by the testator, or by some other person in
his presence and by his direction' (Wills Act 1837, s 9, as substituted
by the Administration of Justice Act 1982, s 17), unless made by
certain soldiers and sailors. This is a formality that cannot be
delegated. There is a special statutory provision which authorises a
person to execute a will on behalf of a mental patient, under an order
of the Court of Protection (Mental Health Act 1983, s 97).

(e) Gifts

There are limits on the authority of an attorney appointed under an
enduring power of attorney to make gifts from the donor's estate
(pp 14–15).

(f) Rules of court

Rules of court may require an act in the course of proceedings to be
done by a specified person, with the result that it cannot be delegated.
This was the case with the signature of a memorandum of appearance
and now presumably with an acknowledgment of service.

In *Re Vic Groves & Co Ltd* [1964] 1 WLR 956, the affidavit in
support of a winding up petition presented by a company was sworn
by a manager of the company under a power of attorney executed by
his employer. This was not accepted, as the rule required an affidavit
by a director, secretary or other principal officer. Again, the
defendant in a probate action was held not to have complied with an
order to serve a list of documents verified by an affidavit, when the
affidavit was sworn by an attorney (*Clauss* v *Pir* [1988] Ch 267).
However, this is not an absolute rule. In exceptional cases, an
attorney's affidavit suffices (*Re African Farms Ltd* [1906] 1 Ch 640: the
attorney actually knew more about the facts than the petitioner, who
was out of the country).

A question which does not seem to have been conclusively settled is
whether a litigant can appoint an attorney to represent him in court,

exercising the donor's right to appear in person. To allow this would be to drive a coach and horses through the traditional monopoly of the legal profession to appear on behalf of litigants. It seems unlikely that a court would accept this.

Chapter 2

Scope of Power

1 Principles

What acts a power of attorney authorises the attorney to do is a question of construction of the document. 'Where an act purporting to be done under a power of attorney is challenged as being in excess of the authority conferred by the power, it is necessary to shew that on a fair construction of the whole instrument the authority in question is to be found within the four corners of the instrument, either in express terms or by necessary implication' (*Bryant, Powis and Bryant Ltd* v *La Banque du Peuple* [1893] AC 170, 177 per Lord Macnaghten).

In considering the extent of powers to be granted, the intending donor should be warned of two contradictory dangers. On the one hand, in conferring unnecessarily wide powers there is the risk that an attorney who turns out to be untrustworthy, or merely one whose judgment is faulty, will exercise his authority in areas which he could and should have left alone. On the other hand, a very restrictive definition of the powers can prevent an attorney from satisfactorily completing the main object of the grant, because he lacks authority to perform necessary acts.

These considerations are obviously more acute in the case of an enduring power of attorney, which will operate after the donor is powerless to change the identity of the attorney or the scope of his authority.

2 Wide powers

(a) Ordinary powers

A donor who wishes to invest his attorney with full powers can seek to itemise and define all the acts that the attorney may do for him, or he may adopt the brief statutory form set out in Schedule 1 to the 1971 Act. The second course is now normally adopted.

The statutory form describes itself as a 'general power of attorney' and simply appoints one person, or more than one, to be the grantor's attorney 'in accordance with section 10 of the Powers of Attorney Act 1971'. A form 'to the like effect', also expressed to be made under the Act, can be used (1971 Act, s 10(1)). Prints of the statutory form are available from stationers.

The statutory form of power authorises the attorney 'to do on behalf of the donor anything which he can lawfully do by an attorney' (1971 Act, s 10(1)). To this, there are certain exceptions. The power does not extend to the functions that the donor has as a trustee or personal representative, or as tenant for life or statutory owners under the Settled Land Act 1925 (1971 Act, s 10(2)). There seems no reason against incorporating into a single document both the statutory form and authority to perform any of the excluded acts that are required in any particular case.

Where an attorney is likely to have to act abroad under the power, it may be more satisfactory to set out the attorney's authority in extenso. Those to whom it has to be exhibited to establish the validity of the attorney's acts may not be aware of the terms of the 1971 Act and may not have the facilities for referring to it.

(b) Enduring powers

There is a prescribed form for creating an enduring power of attorney (1985 Act, s 2(2); Prescribed Form Regulations, Schedule). It incorporates extensive notes, which are an essential part of the form.

There have now been three editions of the prescribed form. The first (Enduring Powers of Attorney (Prescribed Form) Regulations 1986, Schedule) applied to powers granted between 10 March 1986 and 30 June 1988. The second was available for use from 1 November 1987 to 31 July 1991 (Enduring Powers of Attorney (Prescribed Form) Regulations 1987, Schedule). The statutory instruments prescribing the forms are reprinted in Appendix 2. Although the first form can no longer be used to grant new powers, and the second one will shortly be obsolete, they will be relevant for many years to come when considering the validity of older powers. They are therefore referred to below.

In using the statutory form, there are a number of alternatives between which the draftsman must choose, and other adaptations he can make. The power may in the first place, grant 'general authority', which means authority to do anything which the donor can lawfully do by an attorney. This is subject to any qualifications which the instrument contains, and to the limits on the statutory power to make gifts (1985 Act, s 3(2)). The alternative is that the power is limited to specific acts specified in the power. Even then, if the intention is to restrict the statutory powers of the attorney to exercise the donor's trust powers, to benefit himself and to make gifts (1985 Act, s 3(3)–(5)), it is best to impose the limits expressly, as the mere listing of other powers is not likely to be construed as a restriction on the implied powers.

If the power is to be granted to more than one attorney it is essential to specify whether they are to act jointly, or jointly and severally. If no indication is given, the power is not a valid enduring power (1985 Act, s 11(1)).

Additions can be made to the prescribed form, eg to limit the period for which the power is to operate. However, there are certain terms which cannot validly be added:

(1) A right for the attorney to appoint a substitute or successor. That addition prevents the instrument from creating an enduring power (1985 Act, s 2(9));

(2) A term that the power shall continue notwithstanding the attorney's bankruptcy. The bankruptcy automatically revokes the power (1985 Act, s 2(10)). If there is more than one attorney, the bankruptcy of any joint attorney revokes the power. If attorneys are to act jointly and severally, the bankruptcy of any one of them causes him to cease to be an attorney, but only the bankruptcy of the last remaining attorney revokes the power (1985 Act, Sch 3, paras 2, 7).

3 Restricted powers

(a) Generally

An attorney's authority can be limited in a variety of ways: to a particular transaction, eg buying an identified house; to one type of action, eg to collecting rents; to dealing with one named person, eg, operating an account at a specified bank; to a limited period of time. Precedents for clauses to give a power in a variety of specified circumstances are set out in Appendix 4.

A power of attorney given for limited purposes is strictly interpreted by the courts, so that forethought in deciding what is needed and precision in drafting are more important. Examples of reported restrictive interpretations are given below (pp 12–13).

A donor is in a vulnerable position. Although he may hedge the attorney's authority about with restrictions, third parties are entitled to rely upon the attorney's ostensible authority (pp 16).

One way in which the donor can seek to protect himself is to require the attorney always to act explicitly as the donor's agent, and not in his own name. This draws to the attention of third parties the fact that the attorney's authority may be limited. It has express statutory consequences in the case of bills of exchange (p 65). The donor must necessarily still rely on the attorney following his instructions.

Another way in which the donor may seek to safeguard his position is to impose the requirement that the attorney obtain the consent of a named person before acting or before taking any more important steps. Such a limitation is valid, except that in the case of an enduring power statute overrides any requirement of consent in exercising trustee powers, or when making gifts (1985 Act, s 3(3)–(5); p 9). Even where the consent requirement operates without restriction it may cause practical difficulties. A third party dealing with the attorney will require the consent of the person named to be proved, and there is no established routine for that. Again, the power of attorney may effectively be invalidated by the death or incapacity of the named person.

A donor who considers that the concurrence of a named person is essential might just as well appoint that person as joint attorney, but not a joint and several attorney. This will immediately make clear to third parties that his concurrence is necessary.

It is quite possible for the donor to make it a condition that the attorney obtain his (the donor's) concurrence before doing either anything or specific acts. That gives him close control, but defeats the normal purpose of granting a power of attorney which is to allow the attorney to attend to the donor's business without troubling him.

Two points need to be noted in connection with enduring powers of attorney. First, the attorney can probably ignore a requirement that the donor consent to his exercising the power to make gifts. Secondly, once it has been registered, the donor's consent is not effective (1985 Act, s 7(1)(c)), but the Court of Protection may give consent in his stead (s 8(2)(d)). Application is by letter, unless the court otherwise directs, when Form EP3 must be used (Court Rules, r 7(1)). The letter must contain the applicant's name and address and the donor's name, and state the form of relief or determination required and the grounds for the application (r 9(2)). The court may also do this if it has reason to believe that the donor is becoming, or has become, mentally incapable (s 5).

(b) Borrowing

A particular example of the court's policy of construing powers of attorney restrictively is provided by powers to borrow on the donor's behalf. They tend to lean against interpreting a clause as allowing the attorney to borrow and give security from the donor's property (eg *Jacobs* v *Morris* [1902] 1 Ch 816). If the donor wishes the attorney to have this power, it should be expressly stated.

(c) Bank accounts

There is a temptation when a power of attorney is granted for limited purposes to give authority to operate the donor's bank account 'for the purposes aforesaid'. This may result in grave practical inconveniences. The bank may require the attorney to provide strict proof of the purposes for which he wishes to draw money, on each occasion that he does so (*Reckitt* v *Barnett, Pembroke and Slater Ltd* [1929] AC 176).

The easiest way to give the attorney limited access to the donor's bank balance without the inconvenience of additional formalities is usually to open a special account as the only one on which the attorney is entitled to draw.

(d) Examples

The following are examples of powers that have been interpreted restrictively.

POWER CONFERRED	HELD NOT TO AUTHORISE
'To act on my behalf in all matters relating to my property . . . and to mortgage . . .'	Mortgage to secure past debt of donor for that would amount merely to voluntary gift.

Re Bowles' Mortgage Trust (1874) 31 LT 365.

'In connection with my business to make, draw, sign, accept or indorse bills of exchange . . .'	Borrowing money on donor's behalf and giving bills therefor.

Jacobs v *Morris* [1902] 1 Ch 816.

'To settle accounts, pay all debts due from me as executrix of *A* decd, and to act for me as executrix of *A*.'	Accepting bill of exchange for debts due by testator, for that would charge the executrix in her own right.

Gardner v *Baillie* (1796) 6 Term Rep 591.

'To transact all business' (following powers principally to recover specific debts).	Indorsing bill of exchange for discounting.

POWER CONFERRED	HELD NOT TO AUTHORISE

Hay v *Goldsmidt* (1804) 1 Taunt 349; and see *Hogg* v *Snaith* (1808)
1 Taunt 347; *Esdaile* v *La Nauze* (1835) 1 Y&C Ex 394.

'To sign acceptances . . . negotiate, make sale, dispose of, assign and transfer' Government promissory notes.	Pledging the notes.

Jonmenjoy Coondoo v *Watson* (1884) 9 App Cas 561 (PC), distinguishing
Bank of Bengal v *Macleod* (1849) 7 Moo PC 35, where a similar power
included the word 'indorse' and this was held to authorise a pledge.

'To draw cheques without restriction.'	Drawing cheques for donee's private debt.

Reckitt v *Barnett, Pembroke and Slater Ltd* [1929] AC 176.

'For the purpose of exercising for me all . . . powers of privileges conferred by' a partnership deed 'to do anything whatsoever in or about my concerns.'	Dissolving the partnership.

Harper v *Godsell* (1870) LR 5 QB 422.

'To sell all or any of my lands.'	Sale of land previously settled voluntarily on trustees.

General Meat Supply Assocn Ltd v *Bouffler* (1879) 41 LT 719.

'To sell any real or personal property . . . belonging to me.'	Sale of land of which donor was mortgagee.

Re Dowson & Jenkins' Contract [1904] 2 Ch 219.

'To sell and convey my property at *B*, whether owned solely or jointly with any other person.'	Conveyance of land held by donor as trustee for sale.

Green v *Whitehead* [1930] 1 Ch 38 (CA).

4 Gifts

(a) Ordinary powers

An attorney under an ordinary power of attorney can make gifts out of the donor's estate, to the extent that he honestly considers that in doing so he is implementing the purposes for which the power was granted. However, that does not mean that he can make gifts in his own favour, unless the donor expressly authorises it. An attorney's position is in some ways fiduciary, and there is a general rule that a trustee may not benefit from his trust. An attorney is not in every way equated with a trustee—it is accepted practice, eg, for professional attorneys to pay their own fees from the donor's estate, without express authority in the power—yet it is assumed that he cannot make voluntary payments in his own favour.

(b) Enduring powers

Under an enduring power of attorney, even before the time for registration, the position is different: the extent to which the attorney may make gifts is limited, but he is allowed to make them to himself (1985 Act, s 3(4), (5)). This statutory authority operates subject to any conditions or restrictions in the power of attorney, so it can be curbed or completely negatived. To the extent that it does operate, it allows the attorney to act 'without obtaining any consent'.

Precedents for clauses excluding or restricting the statutory power to make gifts are included in Appendix 4.

On the face of it, the Act could be self-contradictory. First, it allows the power of attorney to impose conditions, which certainly might include the need to obtain someone's consent. Then, it says that the authorised gifts may be made without obtaining any consent.

The Law Commission report suggested that this provision was concerned with the consent of the donor (para 4.23). However, the Act is not in any way limited, and applies to all consents. It is suggested that, to give weight to all the words in the Act, it must be assumed that the power to impose conditions and restrictions on the ability to make gifts applies only to the extent that they do not require any consent to be given.

The 1985 Act permits two categories of gift. The first is to provide for persons for whom the donor might be expected to provide. This is interpreted on the assumption that the donor has full mental capacity (s 13(2)). The class, expressly, may include the attorney. In benefiting any such person, the attorney may 'do whatever the donor might be expected to do to meet [his] needs'. This authority may easily extend to such items as paying a regular allowance, providing a home, or paying school or nursing home fees.

Whether or not a person falls within the category of those for whom the donor might be expected to provide is not to be judged by an objective standard, but subjectively by taking into account the actual views of the donor. Equivalent words in s 102(1) (c) of the Mental Health Act 1959 (now Mental Health Act 1983, s 95(1) (c)) were interpreted by Megarry V-C in Re D(J) [1982] Ch 237. He said (p 43),

I think that this provision . . . contemplates the particular patient . . . Before losing testamentary capacity the patient may have been a person with strong antipathies or deep affections for particular persons or causes, or with vigorous religious or political views; and of course the patient was then able to give effect to those views when making a will. I think the court must take the patient as he or she was before losing testamentary capacity. No doubt allowance may be made for the passage of years since the patient was last of full capacity, for sometimes strong feelings mellow into indifference, and even family feuds evaporate. Furthermore, I do not think that the court should give effect to antipathies or affections of the patient which are beyond reason. But subject to all due allowances, I think the court must seek to make a will which the actual patient, acting reasonably, would have made if notionally restored to full mental capacity, memory and foresight.

Even in cases to which this authority for an attorney to benefit himself or others does not apply, he still may be able to do so. The Court of Protection has jurisdiction to authorise an attorney to benefit himself in other cases (1985 Act, s 8(2) (e)). However, its jurisdiction to make directions (s 8(2) (b)) does not extend to authorising gratuitous payments (*Re R (Enduring Power of Attorney)* [1989] 2 WLR 1219).

Application to the court is by letter, unless the court otherwise directs, in which case Form EP3 must be used (Court Rules, r 7(1)). The letter must contain the applicant's name and address and the donor's name, and state the form of relief or determination required and the grounds for the application (r 9(2)).

5 Powers of trustee

A trustee may appoint an attorney to carry out his functions as trustee. Special rules have until now applied as to the extent and manner in which this may be done (Trustee Act 1925, s 25) but an enduring power of attorney can now also be employed (1985 Act, s 3(3)). This is dealt with in detail on pp 27–33.

6 Interpretation

To ascertain the extent of the authority granted by a power of attorney, the words of the document must be construed. The donor's intentions are relevant only to the extent that they are expressed in the deed's terms. As with the interpretation of other documents, this is a matter of law rather than fact.

(a) Donor's ability to perform

No one may delegate the performance of an act which he is not himself entitled to perform. A power of attorney cannot validly authorise the attorney to do a criminal act, nor to perform a contract that is illegal, eg, by being in restraint of trade. The first question to be asked, therefore, to determine whether an attorney has the right to do a particular act is whether the donor has the right to do it (*Shrewsbury & Birmingham Railway Co* v *NW Railway Co* (1857) 6 HL Cas 113).

(b) Ostensible authority

Because, opposite third parties, the attorney's powers extend as far as his ostensible authority (pp 85–87), the donor cannot successfully claim to restrict their scope by relying on private instructions to the attorney (*Bryant, Powis and Bryant Ltd* v *La Banque du Peuple* [1893] AC 170, 180). However, a restriction brought to the attention of third parties is valid (*Overbrooke Estates Ltd* v *Glencombe Properties Ltd* [1974] 1 WLR 1335: printed particulars of a property to be sold by auction gave notice that the auctioneers had no authority to make representations or give warranties about the property).

This rule may be modified where the circumstances put the third party on enquiry. He cannot rely on the attorney's ostensible authority to extend his actual authority as a defence against the consequences of his own negligence. A bank was affected with notice of a donee's abuse of powers when it did not enquire into the circumstances in which he paid into his own account cheques which showed on their face that the money was not his (*Midland Bank Ltd* v *Reckitt* [1933] AC 1).

(c) Recitals

Where a power of attorney contains recitals, which is not now usual, they may limit the scope of the authority that the operative part of the deed grants. A power of attorney that recited the donor's intention of going abroad was held to be effective only during the donor's absence, notwithstanding that the clause conferring the powers contained no such limit (*Danby* v *Coutts & Co* (1885) 29 Ch 500).

(d) General rules of construction

In the interpretation of a power of attorney as for other deeds, statute applies general rules of interpretation. 'Month' means calendar month; 'person' includes a corporation; the singular includes the plural and vice versa; the masculine includes the feminine and vice versa. These meanings can be excluded or modified expressly or by implication if the context requires (Law of Property Act 1925, s 61). However, 'person' and 'individual' are not synonymous. The latter, used in the 1985 Act, only refers to a human person.

(e) Ejusdem generis

The ejusdem generis rule, that general words at the end of a list of items in an identifiable category are construed so as not to extend the category so identified, has been applied to limit the effect of a clause in a power of attorney giving general powers following a series of limited powers (*Bryant, Powis and Bryant Ltd* v *La Banque du Peuple* [1893] AC 170). A general power that stands alone is not affected. A donor who wishes to spell out certain express powers and to follow with a comprehensive power can ensure that the latter is effective by expressing it to be unrestricted by the limitations in previous clauses.

In applying the rule, the court may be affected by the purpose for which the power was granted. 'The power of attorney appoints [the attorney] the purchasing agent for the business carried on by [the donor], and gives him certain particularised powers in connection with purchases, and then goes on to give him this power of accepting bills and making notes in connection with the said business. In my judgment the later words are intended merely to cover such powers beyond the mere power to purchase, which is expressly given, as are necessarily implied by the appointment of [the attorney] as purchasing agent' (*Jacobs* v *Morris* [1902] 1 Ch 816, 828 per Vaughan Williams LJ).

(f) Ambiguity

If a power is ambiguous, the donor is bound when the attorney bona fide places a reasonable interpretation on it and acts accordingly. However, if he acts in a way that does not comply with either possible interpretation, the donor is not bound by the attorney's acts (*Weigall & Co* v *Runciman & Co* (1916) 115 LT 61).

(g) Enduring powers of attorney

An enduring power of attorney can be expressed to confer general authority on the attorney. Subject to any conditions or restrictions in the instrument, and any general rules about gifts applying to enduring powers, this authorises him to do on the donor's behalf anything which the donor can do by an attorney. That is the same formula as is used for the 1971 Act statutory powers.

The Court of Protection has jurisdiction to determine any question as to the meaning of an enduring power of attorney once it has been registered, or earlier if the court has reason to believe that the donor is becoming, or has become, mentally incapable (1985 Act, ss 5, 8(2)(*a*)). Before applying to register a power, the attorney may ask the court to determine any question as to the power's validity (s 4(5)). In either case, the application to the court is by letter, unless the court otherwise directs, when Form EP3 must be used (Court Rules, r 7(1)). The letter must contain the applicant's name and address and the donor's name, and state the form of relief or determination required and the grounds for the application (r 9(2)).

(h) Proper law

At common law the proper law of a power of attorney is the law of the place in which the power is used, or the proper law of the transaction in which it is employed (*Sinfra Akt* v *Sinfra Ltd* [1939] 2 All ER 675). The position under statute must also be considered (see below).

This rule may be modified by the intention of the parties gathered from the instrument. They may therefore expressly elect what the proper law is to be, or their intention may be deduced from the terms of the instrument generally. For example, the adoption of the statutory general power of attorney, with its express reference to the 1971 Act, or the use of an enduring power, will normally imply the adoption of the law of England. (The relevant provisions of the 1971 and 1985 Acts do not extend to Scotland or Northern Ireland.)

Where the proper law of a power of attorney is a foreign law, advice should be sought on the terms of that law both as to the form that a power of attorney should take and as to its interpretation and effect. The rule given above for ascertaining the proper law is the rule of English law. The law of a foreign country where the power is to be used may, of course, reach a different conclusion, or it may impose procedural requirements in respect of all powers of attorney whatever their proper law.

The complications inherent in a proposal to grant a single power of attorney for use in a number of different jurisdictions are obvious. It will often be simpler to prepare a series of separate documents, each for a different country.

The impact of the Contracts (Applicable Law) Act 1990 (not yet brought into force) must also be considered. It implements the 1980 Rome Convention and two other international agreements to which the United Kingdom is a signatory. The Convention (set out in Sch 1 to the Act) does not apply to the question whether, opposite a third party, an attorney can bind the donor (art 1, para 2 (f)). However, it will affect other matters, eg the relations between donor and attorney. An express choice of law is effective (art 3, para 1), unless all the relevant factors are then connected to another single country whose rules will then apply (art 3, para 3). In the absence of a choice by the parties, the proper law will be that of the country with which the power is most closely connected, with a presumption in favour of the attorney's place of residence (art 4, paras 1, 2).

7 Later extensions

(a) Ordinary powers of attorney

A question arises whether, once a power of attorney has been granted, the donor can subsequently informally extend the attorney's authority simply by giving him written instructions.

Section 1 of the 1971 Act casts some doubt on the efficacy of this procedure. That section requires every instrument creating a power of attorney to be executed as a deed. Can it be said that a letter of extension is not a power of attorney, a term not defined by the Act? Although such a letter would not purport to be a power of attorney, it is suggested that any document purporting to confer a new power of this nature should come within the meaning of the term, even though informal. If that is correct, the informality of a letter would render it ineffective, unless it was saved by the doctrine of estoppel preventing the donor from denying that the extension of the authority was effective (p 48).

A later letter can estop the donor from denying that the attorney has authority to do what it requests. If a power gives express authority to do a particular act, and that is followed by general words which would not normally authorise the attorney to go beyond what was necessary for the specified act, a letter from the donor indicating what he wants done can prevent his later denying that the attorney has authority to do it (*Perry* v *Hall* (1860) 2 DeG F & J 38).

An alternative way to achieve an extension of the attorney's authority is to notify a third party that the power is to be treated as extended. In *Reckitt* v *Barnett, Pembroke and Slater Ltd* [1929] AC 176, the donor wrote to his bank saying that they were to treat a power of attorney, which did not expressly refer to drawing cheques, as authorising the attorney to draw on the donor's bank account without restriction. That letter was construed as one with the power and interpreted to mean that cheques could freely be drawn only for the purposes for which the power was given.

A similar letter would clearly still be effective, notwithstanding the 1971 Act, because a bank has a contractual duty to act on its customer's instructions. However, whether a valid estoppel can still be based upon such a letter, if the recipient is not bound to act at the donor's direction, is open to question. If the statement is, on the face of it, invalid in form—as a power of attorney not a deed now is—it seems unlikely that anyone changing his position in reliance upon it would be entitled to protection in the absence of some degree of deceit.

As to the use of subsequent communications to restrict rather than to extend, the attorney's authority, see p 86.

(b) Enduring powers of attorney

Once an enduring power of attorney is registered, the donor cannot extend the scope of the authority which it confers (1985 Act, s 7(1)(c)), even if he is not, at the time he wishes to do so, mentally incapable (s 7(2)). Before an enduring power is registered, the rules relating to an ordinary power apply to it.

Chapter 3

Donor

1 Capacity

The legal capacity to grant a power of attorney generally coincides with the ability of the donor to enter into a binding contract. The rule is that the donor must, with the assistance of whatever explanation he was given, have the mental capacity to understand the nature and effect of the transaction (*Re K, Re F* [1988] Ch 310). This is a common law rule, and none of the statutes dealing with powers of attorney has addressed the point.

For an enduring power, Hoffman J accepted this summary of what the donor must understand when granting it (*Re K, Re F* p 316):

First, if such be the terms of the power, that the attorney will be able to assume complete authority over the donor's affairs; second, if such be the terms of the power, that the attorney will in general be able to do anything with the donor's property which he himself could have done; third, that the authority will continue if the donor should be or become mentally incapable; fourth, that if he should be or become mentally incapable, the power will be irrevocable without confirmation by the court.

A power granted by a donor who lacks capacity can later be validated, if he later regains capacity and then ratifies it. In effect, the original power is a nullity and the power is first effectively granted on the later ratification. The details of the power then granted are ascertained by referring to the original document.

This capacity to grant a valid power must not be confused with the requirement of mental capacity in the donor at the time when the attorney acts under the power (except in the case of enduring powers), see below under *Mental Patients*, p 24.

2 Partners

As a normal partnership is unincorporated, a firm which wishes to appoint an attorney to act on its behalf must do so by means of a joint appointment by all the partners. Their capacity to appoint an attorney jointly is the same as their capacity as individuals. One partner has no implied authority to bind the other partner by deed (*Marchant* v *Morton Down & Co* [1901] 2 KB 829), and as a power of attorney must be given by deed (1971 Act, s 1), one partner cannot grant a valid power of attorney on behalf of the firm.

In relation to any real property which the partners own as partnership property, they (or some of them) will necessarily hold the legal estate as trustees (Law of Property Act 1925, s 34). The rules relating to trustees granting powers of attorney therefore apply (pp 27–33).

There is some theoretical possibility that a firm can create an enduring power of attorney, but the point is unlikely to arise in practice. The donor must be 'an individual' (1985 Act, s 1(1)), which makes it clear that a corporation cannot grant one. But the use of the singular cannot conclusively rule out a power granted by more than one person. When dealing with the attorney, rather than the donor, the Act itself states that unless a trust corporation is appointed, he is to be 'an individual' (s 2(7) (*a*)), but it then goes on to make provision for the appointment of joint attorneys. However, the mechanism of the Act, which turns on whether the donor is or is not becoming mentally incapable, cannot sensibly be operated if there is more than one donor. It is therefore suggested that a firm does not have capacity to create an enduring power.

If one partner grants his copartner a power of attorney to do something which each partner is already entitled to do individually on behalf of the firm—eg, in the case of a trading partnership, to draw and indorse bills of exchange—it is construed as authority to do the act in respect of the partner's personal estate (*Attwood* v *Munnings* (1827) 7 B&C 278).

A partner may be able to delegate his functions as such, although that could well depend on the nature of the partnership and whether it should be inferred that personal performance is one of the partnership obligations. Authority to exercise the donor's powers and privileges under a partnership deed does not permit the attorney to dissolve the partnership (*Harper* v *Godsell* (1870) LR 5 QB 422).

3 Corporations

A corporation cannot grant an enduring power of attorney (1985 Act, s 1(1)). The capacity of a corporation to create an ordinary power of attorney formerly depended on its having the power to do so under its constitution. Even if its constitution gave it the power, it could not validly exercise it by appointing an attorney to do an act which would be ultra vires if it did it itself (*Montreal Assurance Co* v *M'Gillivray* (1859) 13 Moo PC 87). Now, however, no act of a company can be called into question by reason of its lack of capacity, and anyone dealing with a company in good faith may assume that the board of directors are free to bind the company without hesitation (Companies Act 1985, ss 35, 35A; Companies Act 1989, s 108).

The directors of a company may appoint an agent to execute any agreement or instrument which is not a deed in relation to any matters within its powers. This appointment need not be by a formal power of attorney, but can be by resolution or otherwise (Law of Property Act 1925, s 74(2)).

A company has a general power to appoint an attorney to execute deeds on its behalf outside the United Kingdom. A deed which the attorney has executed takes effect as if it were executed under the company's common seal (Companies Act 1985, s 38; Companies Act 1989, Sch 17, para 1). A very full power to appoint attorneys was included in the model form of articles of association in Table A to the 1948 Act but not repeated in the articles in Table A prescribed under the Companies Act 1985 (Companies (Tables A to F) Regulations 1985). The latest form gives a general power for the directors to appoint agents, which may be exercised by granting a power of attorney (art 71).

The 1948 version applied to all companies limited by shares and incorporated between 30 June 1948 and 30 June 1985, unless they adopted special articles of association. The directors may at any time appoint any person, firm or company as attorney for the company. The only limit is that the authority conferred by the power of attorney is that vested in or exercisable by the directors (art 81). That restriction would mean, for example, that no attorney could validly borrow money on the company's behalf in excess of any sum authorised by art 79 if that article applied.

4 Minors

The extent to which a minor (under the age of eighteen: Family Law Reform Act 1969, s 1) can validly grant a power of attorney is still somewhat doubtful. Certainly, it is no longer the case, as Lord Mansfield held, that a power of attorney granted by a minor is void (*Zouch d Abbot and Hallet* v *Parsons* (1765) 3 Burr 1794). Lord Denning MR said, 'The correct proposition is that an infant cannot appoint an agent to make a disposition of his property so as to bind him irrevocably. A disposition by an agent for an infant is voidable just as a disposition by the infant himself would be so long as it is avoided within a reasonable time after attaining full age' (*G(A)* v *G(T)* [1970] 2 QB 643, 652).

There is also the question whether a power of attorney granted by a minor is for that reason revocable in circumstances in which it otherwise would not be. The act of appointing an agent, as distinct from the act of entering into the proposed contract, could itself be an imprudence from the consequences of which the law should protect a minor. However, if the power is coupled with an interest in a transaction that fully binds the minor, there seems no ground for suggesting that it can be revoked. In other cases, the power of attorney itself may be revocable within a reasonable time after the minor comes of age, but without prejudice to the acts already performed under its authority.

The 1985 Act contains no express provision stating whether or not a minor may grant an enduring power of attorney, although it deals with the age of the attorney. The Law Commission report recommended that minors should be able to grant enduring powers (para 4.5). The donor of an enduring power must state his date of birth in the instrument (Prescribed Form Regulations, Schedule), but it is understood that this is merely required by the Court of Protection for administrative reasons.

5 Mental patients

(a) Mental incapacity

The definition of mental incapacity adopted for the purposes of the 1985 Act is that a person 'is incapable by reason of mental disorder of managing and administering his property and affairs' (s 13(1)). 'Mental disorder' means 'mental illness, arrested or incomplete development of mind, psychopathic disorder and any other disorder or disability of mind' (Mental Health Act 1983, s 1(2); 1985 Act, s 13(1)).

The 1985 Act definition of mental incapacity is expressly not applied to cases where a power of attorney is revoked at common law. The 1971 Act refers to revocation by reason of the donor's 'incapacity' (s 4(1) (*a*)(ii)), but attempts no definition.

There is no clear decision as to what constitutes lack of capacity at common law for the purposes of a power of attorney (p 21). It probably follows capacity to contract: 'Was he or she capable of understanding the nature of the contract which he or she entered into?' (*Boughton* v *Knight* (1873) LR 3 P&D 64, 72).

(b) Capacity

A mental patient's capacity to grant a power of attorney is judged by the normal criterion of understanding the nature of the act (p 21). What is relevant is what the donor understands when executing the power. A patient may have a lucid interval and be able to grant a power. There are cases in which a person who is unfit to manage his affairs may nevertheless be able to grant a valid power (*Re K, Re F* [1988] Ch 310).

(c) Validity of attorney's acts

For an act done by an attorney to be valid, the donor must, at common law, have the necessary capacity at two separate times: first when the power is granted, and secondly when the attorney acts. In the latter case, capacity is not merely a question of understanding the attorney's role. An attorney can only validly do an act if, at the time he does it, the donor still has the capacity to do the act in question (*Drew* v *Nunn* (1879) 4 QBD 661).

The common law rule is that subsequent mental incapacity terminates the authority granted by a power, even though the attorney knows nothing of the change in circumstances (*Yonge v Toynbee* [1910] 1 KB 215). There are now, however, a number of exceptions. Attorneys acting under a power which has been revoked without their knowledge have statutory protection (1971 Act, s 5(1)). Opposite third parties, the ostensible authority of an attorney under a revoked power may continue. The donor's mental incapacity will not prejudice the irrevocability of a power coupled with an interest.

6 Drunkards

It seems that if a person who is so drunk that he cannot appreciate what he is doing contracts with another who realises his state, the contract is voidable by the drunkard when he is sober again (*Matthews* v *Baxter* (1873) LR 8 Exch 132). Presumably, the rule would be extended to incapacity because of the influence of narcotic drugs. This should apply on the grant of a power of attorney, on the basis that the capacity to grant a power follows the capacity to contract.

It would not be practical for the authority of an attorney to be cancelled, or even suspended, at any time when the donor happened to be drunk. Yet, in principle, the donor should be of full capacity both when the power is granted, and when authority under it is exercised. The point does not seem to have been decided.

7 Enemy aliens

An enemy alien in time of war cannot validly contract, and therefore is incapable of granting a power of attorney. A power existing when war is declared is automatically revoked when one of the parties becomes an enemy alien (*V/O Sovfracht* v *NV Gebr Van Udens etc* [1943] AC 203).

An irrevocable power of attorney for the sale of land is an exception (*Tingley* v *Muller* [1917] 2 Ch 144). It is suggested that the exception would extend to all powers coupled with an interest, because in such cases the attorney is not really the donor's agent, but acts independently of him.

8 Attorneys

A person who is appointed someone else's attorney normally has no power to grant a further power of attorney, to authorise someone else to carry out his functions under the first power of attorney. The rule *delegatus non potest delegare* makes a subsequent delegation invalid.

Nevertheless, an ordinary power of attorney may authorise the attorney whom it appoints to appoint a substitute. A precedent for a clause for that purpose is given in Appendix 4. The inclusion of such a clause prevents a power qualifying as an enduring power (1985 Act, s 2(9)).

The statutory powers given to trustees as a body to appoint an attorney to deal with property outside the United Kingdom expressly allow them to give that attorney power to appoint a substitute (Trustee Act 1925, s 23(2)).

The attorney would only be able to appoint a substitute if the trustee chose to include an appropriate clause in the power that they granted to him.

With one exception, the statutory provision authorising individual trustees to delegate their powers for up to twelve months contains no reference to substitutes. It does not seem appropriate for a power of attorney granted thereunder to contain such a clause. It would undermine part of the purpose of the statutory notice of the grant of the power, which has to name the attorney. The exception is to permit the delegation of the power to transfer inscribed stock (Trustee Act 1925, s 25(6)).

9 Trustees: Trustee Act powers

(a) Generally

Trustees are subject to the rule *delegatus non potest delegare*. Accordingly, they have no *prima facie* power to appoint an attorney to carry out their functions. There are certain exceptions to this, dealt with below, where statute authorises trustees to delegate in specific circumstances. They may also delegate purely ministerial functions, which do not involve the exercise of any discretion, to carry into effect the consequences of a discretion already exercised (*Offen v Harman* (1859) 29 LJ Ch 307). This allows the delegation of the receipt of purchase money on the sale of a trust asset (*Re Hetling and Merton's Contract* [1893] 3 Ch 269). Otherwise, a purported delegation by trustees is invalid, whether it relates to express trusts or to statutory trusts (*Green v Whitehead* [1930] 1 Ch 38).

In considering whether trustees' powers can be delegated, one must distinguish between cases where a single trustee wants his responsibilities to be undertaken by someone else, and those cases where all the trustees of a particular settlement wish to delegate the exercise of their functions.

(b) Individual trustees: the Trustee Act

An individual trustee now has two alternative powers to authorise an attorney to carry out his functions as trustee. The first is regulated by the Trustee Act 1925, as amended by the 1971 Act, s 9. The second, and in many respects, wider authority entails the grant of an enduring power of attorney, and is dealt with in the next section.

Under the Trustee Act, a trustee may grant a power of attorney to delegate the execution or exercise of all or any of the trusts, powers and discretions that are vested in him. This ability extends both to cases where he is sole trustee and where he is trustee jointly. The period for which a trustee may delegate his powers is limited: it may not exceed twelve months (Trustee Act 1925, s 25(1)). A power granted under the Trustee Act cannot be an enduring power (1985 Act, s 2(8)).

A trustee donor must comply with a further formality. He has to give notice of the power of attorney to any person, other than himself, who under the trust instrument has the sole or joint power of appointing new trustees and also to any other trustees. He must give the notice before the power of attorney is granted, or within seven days after.

The notice must state:
  (i)   the date the power comes into operation;
  (ii) its duration;
  (iii) the identity of the attorney;
  (iv) the reason for granting the power;
  (v)   what trusts, powers and discretions are delegated, unless they all are.

Failure to give notice, or the giving of a deficient one, does not invalidate any act done by the attorney or any instrument executed by him as far as the person dealing with the attorney is concerned. A form of notice for this purpose is set out in Appendix 3.

The Council of the Law Society expressed the opinion in 1931 that the costs of a power of attorney granted by a trustee about to go abroad—which, before the 1971 Act, was the case which the Trustee Act 1925 covered—are properly paid from the trust fund (1 *Law Society's Digest* 480).

The statutory power of delegation may be curtailed by an express prohibition to that effect in the trust instrument (Trustee Act 1925, s 69(2)).

The attorney whom a trustee appoints may be a trust corporation, but he cannot grant a power of attorney to his sole cotrustee, unless that cotrustee is a trust corporation (Trustee Act 1925, s 25(2)). There is no express bar on one trustee appointing as his attorney the person who has already been appointed attorney of all the other trustees, although others have doubted the validity of such an appointment.

Presumably, the one attorney can do the same act on behalf of his different principals. He could thus acknowledge receipt of capital money arising on the sale of land which is the subject of a trust for sale, on behalf of more than one trustee, and the requirement to pay it to at least two trustees would be satisfied so that a purchaser of a legal estate need not be concerned with the trusts affecting the proceeds of sale (Law of Property Act 1925, s 27).

The ban on the donor's sole cotrustee being his attorney is not expressed as a prohibition against the donor *appointing* the cotrustee. Rather, the Act says that the only other cotrustee may not *be* the attorney. That may well mean that the position is not only to be judged at the moment the appointment takes effect, but at all material times. Say there are three trustees, *A*, *B* and *C*. *A* can validly appoint *B* as his attorney. However, if *C* later dies, leaving *B* as *A*'s only cotrustee, that is prohibited and perhaps the power of attorney is then invalidated. This point has not yet been decided.

Although there is a twelve month time limit on a power of attorney granted by a trustee, there is nothing to prevent his granting a succession of such powers. Each time he does so, he must give the required notice. If the reason for granting the powers is the trustee's absence from the United Kingdom for more than twelve months, the notices will serve to draw to the attention of those with the power to appoint new trustees the fact that they are able to exercise their power to replace him (Trustee Act 1925, s 36(1)).

The validity of a power granted by a trustee does not depend on the existence of the circumstances that provided the reason for its creation. If, for example, a power is granted because the trustee is going abroad, its validity is not limited to the period when he is outside the country. On the contrary, the power comes into force as soon as it is executed, or later if it is expressed to take effect later.

The trustee's own authority is not cancelled by the delegation. In this as in other cases, the donor's powers and those of the attorney subsist concurrently.

(c) Trustees as a body

Trustees collectively are authorised by statute to appoint an attorney for dealing with trust property, of any kind, outside the United Kingdom. This is a power to 'appoint any person to act as their agent or attorney for the purpose of selling, converting, collecting, getting in, and executing and perfecting insurances [a misprint for 'assurances': *Green* v *Whitehead* [1930] 1 Ch 38, 45 per Eve J] of, or managing or cultivating, or otherwise administering any property, real or personal, moveable or immoveable, subject to the trust or forming part of the testator's or intestate's estate, in any place outside the United Kingdom or executing or exercising any discretion or trust or power vested in them in relation to any such property, with such ancillary powers, and with and subject to any provisions and restrictions as they may think fit, including a power to appoint substitutes' (Trustee Act 1925, s 23(2)). The trustees are not, by reason only of their having made such an appointment, responsible for any loss that arises.

It is only the property to which a power of attorney granted under this provision relates that must be outside the United Kingdom.

Where appropriate, the trustees may appoint an attorney who is himself in the United Kingdom.

Trustees also have a general authority to employ and pay agents, including professional advisers, 'to transact any business or do any act required to be transacted or done in the execution of the trust' (Trustee Act 1925, s 23(1)). This does not permit trustees to delegate their discretions and management responsibilities, but merely to charge to the trust fund the cost of obtaining professional assistance to do what they might otherwise have done themselves.

(d) Trustees for sale

Trustees for the sale of land are, in principle, in the same position in relation to the delegation of their functions as are other trustees. There are, however, some exceptional cases.

Trustees for sale may delegate leasing powers to any person of full age beneficially entitled in possession to the net rents and profits of land for life or any lesser period, but not merely as an annuitant. The powers in question are those of and incidental to leasing, accepting surrenders of leases and management. The delegation must be revocable, but may extend until the sale of the land. The only formality needed is writing signed by the trustees (Law of Property Act 1925, s 29).

The delegated leasing powers are exercised in the name of the trustees. The position of tenants is protected, unless some irregularity is apparent. Normally, the written instrument is sufficient evidence of the identity of the person to whom powers have been delegated. Its production is sufficient evidence that it has not been revoked. The beneficiary exercising the leasing powers has the duties and liabilities of a trustee, and his acts and defaults do not render the trustees liable.

Where one of two joint owners wants to appoint an attorney to effect a sale, he cannot effectively do so by a power to sell his property 'whether owned solely or jointly with any other person' (*Green* v *Whitehead* [1930] 1 Ch 38). He must therefore use his trustee's power of delegation, which means that he cannot appoint his cotrustee as his attorney, unless the cotrustee is a trust corporation (Trustee Act 1925, s 25(2); 1971 Act, s 9(2)), or grant an enduring power of attorney. The 1971 Act statutory form is not applicable (*Walia* v *Michael Naughton Ltd* [1985] 1 WLR 1115).

(e) Charitable trustees

To avoid the difficulties that can stem from the fact that the number of trustees of a charity is not limited to four, special legislation allows them to delegate authority to execute deeds and instruments to at least two of their number (Charities Act 1960, s 34). This power can be modified or cancelled by the trusts of the charity. A deed is not necessary to exercise this power. The delegation can be in writing, or by a resolution of the trustees.

The trustees to execute deeds can be designated in a number of ways, eg: any, say, two trustees; certain named trustees, or a particular number selected from a list of names; at least one trustee nominated or appointed by each of two separate appointors. There is no restriction on the way they are selected, but it should be done so as to make it clear to third parties dealing with the trustees that the requirements have been fulfilled.

A person who in good faith acquires for money or money's worth an interest in or charge on property, or the benefit of any covenant or agreement expressed to be entered into by the charitable trustees, is protected. If the deed or instrument purports to be executed under this power, it is conclusively presumed to have been duly executed. However, the requirement of 'good faith' on the part of the person relying on the delegated authority will generally mean at least of the person who originally dealt directly with the trustees, that he must make reasonable enquiries to satisfy himself of the terms of the delegation, and that they have been observed.

Once authority has been given under the provision, and unless it is revoked or lapses under conditions imposed when it was created, it continues notwithstanding any change of trustees. Delegation to any two trustees can therefore be indefinite. If the trustees to exercise the power are named, the authority will necessarily be limited to the period during which they continue to be trustees, because only a trustee can be authorised to execute deeds and instruments.

10 Trustees: enduring powers

(a) Statutory authority

The attorney under an enduring power of attorney may execute or exercise all or any trusts, powers or discretions vested in the donor as trustee (1985 Act, s 3(3)). This applies both before and after the power is registered provided the attorney has executed it. Conditions or restrictions in the instrument can curtail or remove this authority, but subject to that the attorney may act without obtaining any consent. The statutory power expressly extends to giving a valid receipt for capital or other money paid.

A precedent for a clause excluding the statutory power is included in Appendix 4.

This provision is extremely wide in scope. Although it was apparently introduced specifically to deal with the case of jointly owned properties, where one of two owners wishes to appoint the other as his attorney, it is of general application. It can be used in respect of any type of trust or settlement. The only respect in which the Trustee Act provisions may be wider is that the 1985 Act refers only to the donor's powers 'as trustee', while the 1925 Act expressly extends to personal represenatives, tenants for life and statutory owners (s 25(8)).

To use an enduring power of attorney is generally much simpler. There is no need for any notice to be given to cotrustees or the person entitled to appoint new trustees. There is no limit on the period for which the power may last. There is no restriction on who may be appointed as attorney. Further, because an enduring power can confer this authority at once, there is no need while the trustee donor is still of full capacity for the registration procedure to operate. Once the power has served its purpose, the donor can revoke it, but if he does so he must remember the need for giving notice of revocation of an enduring power.

A precedent for an enduring power of attorney to delegate a trustee's powers in respect of one or more named trusts is included in Appendix 3.

The simplicity which the use of an enduring power of attorney offers here undermines some safeguards which normally apply when a trustee deals with property. First, the reference to the attorney's ability to give a receipt for capital money is probably intended to authorise one person to give a receipt in two capacities—both as trustee, and as a second trustee's attorney—so as to satisfy the requirement that capital money on the sale of land be paid to at least two trustees. The doubt about the meaning of the provision arises from the fact that a simple appointment as attorney normally authorises the giving of receipts for money on behalf of the donor; something more must therefore be intended. Secondly, the provision allowing the attorney to exercise the donor's trustee powers, without obtaining any consent, overrides any requirement in the trust instrument that consent be obtained before a disposition by the trustees (the effect of which was largely preserved by s 26(1) of the Law Property Act 1925). It can also be argued that where the donor is trustee of a charity, the 1985 Act has dispensed with the need for any consent required under s 29 of the Charities Act 1960.

(b) Mental disorder: trusts for sale of land

Ironically perhaps, an enduring power of attorney granted by a trustee under a trust for sale of land may not be capable of use once the trustee is mentally incapable; it may lose the ability to survive the donor's incapacity which normally distinguishes an enduring power. There is a special statutory provision relating to a trustee for sale who becomes incapable of exercising his functions as trustee 'by reason of mental disorder'. It is conceivable that this position will be reached at a different time from the trustee becoming mentally incapable under the 1985 Act—because the one is concerned with the trustee's ability to exercise his functions *as trustee*, and the other with his ability to manage *his own* affairs—but it seems likely that both provisions will have effect simultaneously.

The rule governing trustees for sale is a mandatory requirement that a new trustee be appointed to replace the trustee who has become incapable (Law of Property Act 1925, s 22(2); Mental Health Act 1959, Sch 7, Pt 1). Clearly, if the trustee is replaced, any power of attorney which he had granted must cease to have effect in relation to that trust. The conclusion must be that as soon as the moment has come when the attorney has a duty to apply for registration of the enduring power, his powers under any trust for sale of land of which the donor was a trustee must cease.

The view has been challenged ((1987) 131 SJ 1509) on the grounds that it would frustrate the purpose of the enactment, and that the later provision must impliedly repeal the earlier one because they are inconsistent. Neither argument is self-evident. The 1985 Act provision was introduced to overcome difficulties created by *Walia* v *Michael Naughten Ltd* [1985] 1 WLR 1115. That was not a case of mental incapacity, so its reversal is not relevant to resolving the statutory conflict. Again, there is not total inconsistency between the two Acts, because the later one can apply without question before the donor trustee becomes incapable. Until the doubt is resolved by litigation or further legislation, the only safe course, once a trustee who has granted a power of attorney becomes mentally incapable, is to doubt its validity even if it is an enduring power.

11 Personal representatives

Once a grant of representation has been made, personal representatives have merely the limited powers of delegation that are enjoyed by trustees generally.

Powers of attorney to obtain grants of representation are dealt with separately in Chapter 16.

12   Tenants for life and statutory owners

The statutory powers that trustees have to delegate, both individually and collectively, apply equally to tenants for life and to statutory owners (Trustee Act 1925, ss 23(1), 25(8); 1971 Act s 9(3)).

There are special provisions about the notice that an individual must give on granting a power of attorney. In the case of a tenant for life, it goes to the trustees of the settlement and to any other person who, jointly with the donor, constitutes the tenant for life. A statutory owner must give notice to any other person who, with the donor, constitutes the statutory owner. A person who is named in the settlement as the person to exercise the powers of a tenant for life, where there is no tenant for life and no person on whom those powers are conferred by statute, and who is thereby tenant for life (Settled Land Act 1925, s 23(1)(a)), also has to give notice to the trustees of the settlement.

13   Bankrupts

While a bankrupt is not barred from granting a power of attorney, it is not of practical importance, at least as far as disposing of property is concerned, because his property is vested in his trustee in bankruptcy.

Upon the donor of an earlier power of attorney becoming bankrupt, the power is automatically revoked (*Markwick* v *Hardingham* (1880) 15 Ch 339). A power coupled with an interest is an exception to this rule, and is not affected (*Barclays Bank Ltd* v *Bird* [1954] Ch 274). It is also possible for an attorney to perform ministerial acts, merely carrying into effect a contract entered into before the bankruptcy (*Dixon* v *Ewart* (1891) Buck 94). An undischarged bankrupt cannot grant an enduring power of attorney (1985 Act, s 2(7)(a)).

14   Trustees in bankruptcy

A trustee in bankruptcy is empowered to execute any power of attorney needed for carrying into effect the provisions of the Insolvency Act 1986 (Sch 5, para 14 (f)). He does so using the title 'the trustee of the estate of [the bankrupt] a bankrupt' (s 305(4)).

15 Liquidators

A liquidator in a winding up has power 'to appoint an agent to do any business which the liquidator is unable to do himself'. The power extends to acts which the liquidator is 'unable' rather than 'unwilling' to do (Insolvency Act 1986, Sch 4, para 12).

Chapter 4

Attorney

1 Capacity

(a) Freedom of choice

Generally, the donor of a power of attorney has complete freedom of choice in deciding who shall act as his attorney. In practice, the selection is obviously important, but, except in the case of an enduring power, the law does not take any special steps to restrict the capacity to act as an attorney to those who might be considered suitable.

(b) Suitability

In the case of an enduring power of attorney, the authority of the attorney can be challenged on the ground that he is unsuitable, but not until the time comes to apply to register the power. On the application for registration, the Court of Protection has power to refuse to register on the ground 'that, having regard to all the circumstances and in particular the attorney's relationship to or connection with the donor, the attorney is unsuitable to be the donor's attorney' (1985 Act, s 6(5)(e)). It can also cancel an earlier registration on that ground (s 8(4)(g)). The unsuitability of any attorney appointed to act jointly is sufficient to enable the court to act (Sch 3, paras 4,6). The Act has no definition of 'relationship' or 'connection' for this purpose. If the court either refuses or cancels a registration on this ground, it makes an order revoking the power and, unless it otherwise directs, the instrument is delivered up to be cancelled (ss 6(7), (8), 8(5), (6)).

2 More than one attorney

If more than one attorney is appointed, the grant of the power may be to them jointly, in which case they may only act together, or to them severally, in which case they can act separately. The 1971 Act statutory form of general power allows, and indeed requires, the donor to choose. An enduring power of attorney which appoints more than one attorney must state whether they are to act jointly, or jointly and severally (1985 Act, s 11(1)). If it does not do so, it cannot be an enduring power, although it could be an ordinary power. In that case, it would still be necessary to determine the status of the attorneys, but this would have to be done by evidence, rather than a statement in the instrument.

There is an essential difference between attorneys appointed to act jointly, and those to act jointly and severally: the authority of those to act jointly can only be exercised collectively, whereas an attorney permitted to act jointly and severally may act either on his own or with the other attorneys. The result is that a joint power must necessarily come to an end when any one of the attorneys ceases to have the capacity to act, or dies. It is then impossible for all of them to act together as the appointment requires.

The position where some, but not all, of the attorneys appointed by what is intended to be an enduring power of attorney qualify as attorneys under such a power is not entirely clear. One of them may, for example, not execute the instrument which is a requirement in the case of an enduring power (1985 Act, s 2(1)(b)). This will not prevent the instrument being an enduring power in respect of the other attorneys, and it can be an ordinary power as far as the one who did not execute is concerned (s 11(4)). No distinction is drawn there between joint powers and joint and several ones, but it would seem that the saving of enduring powers in relation to those attorneys who comply with the creation formalities is not effective where their authority is joint. On the disability of the donor, the power is automatically revoked to the extent that it is an ordinary, not an enduring, power. It is then no longer possible for all the attorneys to exercise their authority together, as a joint appointment requires. The conclusion must be that the saving is effective only for joint and several powers.

An ordinary power could specify that, say, any two of a greater number of attorneys should act on any occasion, but such a requirement would not meet the statutory requirement for enduring powers that the attorneys must be appointed to act either jointly or jointly and severally (1985 Act, s 11(1)). A joint and several power granted to fifteen people was validly exercised by four of them (*Guthrie* v *Armstrong* (1822) 5 B&A 628).

If one of several attorneys disclaims the power, that does not prejudice its exercise by any attorneys that remain, unless the power of attorney provides to the contrary (Law of Property Act 1925, s 156(2)). A provision that a power is to be exercised by all the attorneys jointly would preclude the remaining attorneys acting after one had disclaimed.

3 Minors

A minor can be appointed an attorney and can bind the donor of an ordinary power (*Re D'Angibau* (1880) 15 Ch 228, 246), but only in relation to property other than land (*Hearle* v *Greenbank* (1749) 3 Atk 695). It is not clear whether an attorney who is a minor can merely be appointed to carry out ministerial powers, or to what extent discretion can be delegated to him.

Although a minor cannot own a legal estate in land (Law of Property Act 1925, s 1(6)), there seems no reason why someone under age should not be appointed attorney to deal with land. This could be done before 1926, provided the minor had no interest in the property (*King* v *Bellord* (1863) 1 H&M 343, 347), but there seems to have been no decision since.

An attorney under an enduring power of attorney must be of full age when he executes the instrument (1985 Act, s 2(7)(*a*)). The donor can validly execute a power appointing as his attorney a person who is a minor—subject to the limitations mentioned above—but until the attorney attains the age of eighteen and executes the power, it can only be an ordinary power.

Where an enduring power appoints joint, but not joint and several, attorneys, it is only necessary that every attorney be eighteen when the last of them executes the instrument (Sch 3, para 1). So if *A* (aged seventeen) and *B* (an adult) are appointed attorneys to act jointly, *A*'s appointment and immediate execution become valid, even though he is only seventeen, provided *B* delays executing the power until *A*'s eighteenth birthday. The power is not effective as an enduring power until *B* has executed. Notwithstanding this, the prescribed form requires every attorney to declare when signing: 'I am not a minor'. To this extent the form may be ultra vires.

There is no express requirement that an attorney appointed by a trustee under the Trustee Act should be of full age. However, as a minor cannot be appointed as a trustee (Law of Property Act 1925, s 20), it must be doubtful whether a power of attorney can validly delegate a trustee's discretionary powers to a minor. Such a grant would be repugnant to the statutory restriction on under age trustees.

An attorney appointed to take a grant of letters of administration must be of full age.

4 Trustees

A trustee, other than a trust corporation, cannot validly be appointed the attorney of the only other trustee of the settlement (Trustee Act 1925, s 25(2); 1971 Act, s 9(2)), except by an enduring power of attorney (1985 Act, s 3(3)).

5 Bankrupts

It has been said that the bankruptcy of an attorney under an ordinary power of attorney automatically revokes the power (*Hudson* v *Granger* (1821) 5 B&Ald 27). But that is not universally the case, even where the attorney receives money on the donor's behalf (*McCall* v *The Australian Meat Co Ltd* (1870) 19 WR 188). It now seems that a power is revoked only if the nature of the attorney's duties is such that his bankruptcy renders him unfit to carry them out.

In the case of an enduring power of attorney, the attorney may not be bankrupt when he executes the instrument (1985 Act, s 2(7) (*a*)), and his subsequent bankruptcy revokes the power (s 2(10)). If there is more than one attorney, the effect of one of them becoming bankrupt varies depending whether their authority is joint, or joint and several. The bankruptcy of any joint attorney revokes the power (Sch 3, para 2). If a joint and several attorney is bankrupt, he ceases to be an attorney, leaving the other attorney(s) free to act. On the last attorney becoming bankrupt, the power is revoked (Sch 3, para 7).

6 Corporations

(a) Generally

A corporation can act as attorney if it is authorised to do so by its memorandum of association or other constitution document. In appointing a large corporation, it is common to provide for the attorney to nominate one of its officers to carry out the functions. Or, the power can actually appoint 'such of the officers of Ltd/plc as the company shall appoint' (cf the power cited in *Barclays Bank Ltd* v *Bird* [1954] Ch 274). The only corporation which can be an attorney under an enduring power of attorney is a trust corporation (1985 Act, s 2(7)).

(b) Trust corporations

A trust corporation is designated by statute or statutory instrument. Disregarding those designated for limited purposes only, they include (Law of Property (Amendment) Act 1926, s 3(1); Supreme Court Act 1981, s 128; Public Trustee Rules 1912, r 30 (as amended):

  (1) the Official Solicitor, the Treasury Solicitor, the solicitor to the Duchy of Lancaster;

  (2) the Public Trustee (it is understood that, as a matter of practice, the Public Trustee does not act as attorney);

  (3) a corporation complying with the following conditions:

     (i) it is incorporated under the law of the whole or any part of a member state of the European Economic Community;

    (ii) its constitution empowers it to undertake trust business in England and Wales;

   (iii) it has at least one place of business in the United Kingdom;

   (iv) its constitution comes into one of three categories. First, it is incorporated by special Act of Parliament or Royal Charter. Or, secondly, it is a company, either limited or unlimited, registered in a European Economic Community member state with an issued capital of not less than £250,000 of which at least £100,000 has been paid up in cash. Or, thirdly, it is an unlimited company registered in a European Economic Community member state, and one of its constituent members is a company within one of the first two categories.

7 Partners

The appointment of a partner in a firm as attorney is a personal appointment and confers no authority on any other partner.

There is doubt whether the appointment of a firm as attorney, by its firm name, validly constitutes the partners for the time being the donor's attorneys. In principle, the appointment should be perfectly valid if the reference to the firm's name identifies the individual partners with certainty. In *Re Horgan decd* [1971] P 50, the appointment of a firm of solicitors as executors of a will was construed as referring to the partners in the named firm at the date of the testator's death.

As a power of attorney normally takes effect immediately there ought to be no complication arising from changes of partners. But the questions would arise, as matters of construction, whether the partners were attorneys only so long as they remained partners and whether new partners were to be treated as substitute attorneys.

An enduring power of attorney can only be valid in this form if the members of the firm were expressly appointed either to act jointly or to act jointly and severally (1985 Act, s 11(1)). There is an additional complication in this case. All joint attorneys, or every joint and several attorney who is to be authorised to act under the instrument as an enduring power, must execute it. In this case, there could be no question of substitute attorneys appointed by the original ones (s 2(9)).

If the firm's name alone is used in the power, proof will be needed of the identity of those executing it and possibly evidence of who the partners then were. This cannot be recommended. There seems to be no advantage in not naming the partners in an enduring power.

If the intention is that the attorneys are to be the partners in the firm for the time being, and that the appointment is to continue in relation to the current partners, notwithstanding changes in the firm's constitution, it is recommended that the deed should refer to the partners in the firm (although not named) rather than to the firm itself. An enduring power of attorney could not be drawn on that basis. This type of appointment is subject to considerable drawbacks. At any time, one of the attorneys may be called upon to prove that he is, at the relevant time, a member of the firm in question. The firm may be dissolved, or it may split so that it is not clear which new entity, if any, is the successor to the original partnership. A power of this type should appoint the partners as several attorneys rather than joint ones, as even if the firm is originally small, it may grow to a point where the involvement of all the partners in joint decisions under the power of attorney is impracticable.

A precedent of a clause to appoint the partners for the time being in a named firm as attorneys is included in Appendix 4, but its use is subject to the reservations expressed here.

If a power of attorney is given to one partner not in connection with the business of the firm, the other partners are not liable for any breach of duty of misconduct on the attorney's part. However, if the appointment of one of the partners is in respect of something within the scope of the firm's business—eg the appointment of a partner in a firm of solicitors to execute a conveyance and complete a sale of land, in which the firm was acting professionally for the donor—then the whole firm is responsible for the attorney's acts.

8 Successors in title

A power of attorney coupled with an interest, given to secure a proprietary interest, may be granted to the person entitled to that interest and those deriving title to it under him. Those successors in title automatically become attorneys under the power, by virtue of their title to the property in question (1971 Act, s 4(2)).

A case in which a grant in this form is useful is where the purchaser of land for resale takes a power to execute conveyances in favour of ultimate purchasers (pp 113–114).

Chapter 5

Contents of Power

1 Recitals

A power of attorney may recite the circumstances in which it comes to be executed. This is not usual, and it is rarely advisable. The interpretation of the main provisions of the power can be affected by the recitals, which can reduce the scope of the attorney's authority (*Danby* v *Coutts & Co* (1885) 29 Ch 500). This may mean that those dealing with the attorney have to make more extensive enquiries than usual to assure themselves of the validity of what he proposes to do.

2 Attorney's powers

The extent of the authority of the attorney should be set out in the power, unless either statutory form of power of attorney is adopted. The extent and definition of the powers is discussd in Chapter 2 (p 8).

3 Substitution and delegation

A donor who wants his attorney to be able to appoint a substitute or to delegate any of his duties must include in the power a clause to that effect. This is forbidden in the case of an enduring power (1985 Act, s 2(9)), but see pp 120–121. The 1971 Act form of general power makes no reference to a power to appoint a substitute. The authority it confers on the attorney is 'to do on behalf of the donor anything which he can lawfully do by an attorney' (s 10(1)). The act of appointing a substitute is an act the attorney does by authority of the donor, but not on his behalf. For that reason, it is considered that the statutory form of general power, without more, does not authorise the attorney to appoint a substitute.

The donor can limit the choice of substitute, for example, to another member of the firm in which the attorney is a partner or to a person qualified as a chartered surveyor. This, however, involves the difficulty that a third party could require proof that the substitute qualified for appointment. A compromise is to allow a third party to assume that any substitute does qualify. This prevents the donor from repudiating any of the substitute's acts on the ground that he should not have been appointed. He would have a right of recourse against the attorney if he suffered loss as a result of an improper appointment.

A form of clause for this purpose is included in Appendix 4.

A power coupled with an interest and securing a proprietary interest can be granted to the person entitled to that interest and his successors in title. Those successors become the attorneys, by a form of statutory substitution. However, if the power also includes a clause entitling the attorney to appoint a substitute, that remains effective (1971 Act, s 4(2)).

4 Duration

The power of attorney can define the period for which the attorney's authority is to last. This is discussd further in Chapter 7, p 54.

5 Remuneration of attorney

It is doubted whether the rule that a trustee may not profit from his trust unless expressly authorised to do so is applicable to attorneys. Certainly, a power of attorney can provide for remuneration for the attorney (*Frith* v *Frith* [1906] AC 254). Although there does not seem to be authority on the question whether an attorney can claim payment quantum meruit in the absence of express terms about remuneration, it is suggested that he could. If the attorney acts under a contract that he will provide that service, he will have a claim for a reasonable charge under the Supply of Goods and Services Act 1982, s 15.

That would certainly accord with practice. A large number of powers are granted to professional advisers, without express terms about payment. The understanding, which is fulfilled, is that the attorney will be paid for what he does.

The view that no charging clause is required is supported by an opinion of the Council of the Law Society given in 1958. This states that a solicitor who is appointed an attorney under a power without any express provision about his remuneration is entitled to charge both for his professional work, including the preparation of the power of attorney, and for non-professional work undertaken as attorney (1 *Law Society's Digest*, 4th cum supp 96). A form of clause expressly entitling the attorney to charge is included in Appendix 4.

6 Ratification

(a) General

A power of attorney often contains an undertaking by the donor to ratify what the attorney does or purports to do under the power. The scope of this provision is in some doubt. A clause undertaking to ratify 'whatsoever' the attorney did or purported to do was held not to extend the scope of the authority granted by the power (*Midland Bank Ltd* v *Reckitt* [1933] AC 1).

It is suggested that the true meaning of the clause is to prevent the donor from denying the attorney's authority to do anything which the power appears to permit, even though, because of some irregularity, the attorney was not effectively invested with the necessary powers. In other words, the clause merely reinforces the power, but does not extend it.

It may not even be able to go that far. True ratification is always retrospective. If therefore the donor was not legally capable of performing the act at the date of its performance, so that he could not have delegated the power to perform it, there can be no ratification (*Boston Deep Sea Fishing and Ice Co Ltd* v *Farnham* [1957] 1 WLR 1051). Usually only the principal for whom an act was purported to be done can ratify it. But a receiver for debenture holders has been held capable of ratifying a transaction carried out by an earlier receiver, as no third party rights had intervened (*Lawson* v *Hosemaster Co Ltd* [1966] 1 WLR 1300).

There may be ratification even though the donor has not undertaken to ratify. It can extend to validating acts that were in fact beyond the attorney's authority. Ratification may be deduced from the donor's conduct.

(b) Enduring powers of attorney

Ratification by the donor is not effective once he becomes mentally incapable, and therefore an express covent to ratify is of limited use in an enduring power of attorney.

Once the power has been registered, the Court of Protection has jurisdiction wholly or partly to relieve the attorney from any liability he has or may have incurred on account of a breach of his duties as attorney (1985 Act, s 8(2)(*f*)). It can make such an order before registration if it has reason to believe that the donor is becoming, or has become, mentally incapable (s 5). An order under this provision can have the effect of ratifying an earlier action taken by the attorney. It is to be noted that the court's power extends to liabilities incurred before the power was registered, and before the court acquired jurisdiction by reason of the fact that the time to apply for registration had arrived. Application to the court is by letter, unless it directs that Form EP3 shall be used (Court Rules, r 7(1)). The letter must contain the applicant's name and address and the donor's name, and state the form of relief and determination required and the grounds for the application (r 9(2)).

7 Proper law

A power of attorney may expressly declare which is to be the proper law of the power. This will be effective, at least in English law, to designate the law governing the relations between the donor and the attorney. Whether the power is acceptable in the country in which it is to be used must depend on the law of that country. (As to the impact of the Contracts (Applicable Law) Act 1990, which has yet to be brought into force, see pp 18–19).

Chapter 6

Form of Power

1 Deed

(a) Newly granted powers

A power of attorney must now be granted by deed (1971 Act, s 1). Although this general rule, which was new in 1971, is unqualified, it seems to be accepted that it does not extend to other documents in the nature of powers of attorney that are expressly authorised, for instance, delegation of powers by charitable trustees, appointment of an agent to sign a contract on behalf of a company, or a proxy granted by a shareholder in a company. This may be because these other documents are not to be regarded as powers of attorney for the purposes of the 1971 Act. That Act contains no definition of the term.

The need for a power of attorney to be granted by deed may influence the form of an instrument to which a power is incidental, for example, a memorandum of deposit of title deeds, constituting an informal equitable mortgage of the land, is effective although not a deed. To enable the mortgagee to exercise the statutory power of sale in case of default, a memorandum often incorporates a power of attorney by which the mortgagor appoints the mortgagee his attorney to execute a legal charge. That power can only be valid if the memorandum is a deed.

(b) Older powers

Before 1971, a power of attorney had to be a deed under seal if it authorised the attorney to execute a deed on the donor's behalf or if it was giving more general authority which would necessarily involve that (*Berkeley* v *Hardy* (1826) 5 B&C 355). Similarly, a power to deliver a deed already signed and sealed had to be under seal (*Windsor Refrigerator Co Ltd* v *Branch Nominees Ltd* [1961] Ch 88; rvsd on other grounds). However, a verbal authority sufficed to allow an

47

attorney to execute a deed in the donor's presence (*R* v *Longnor (Inhabitants)* (1833) 4 B&Ad 647).

In one case, a guarantee was effectively executed by an attorney, even though the power had not been sealed. The power stated that it had been 'signed, sealed and delivered' in the presence of the witness, and the seal had apparently been omitted by an oversight. A bank advanced money on security of a debenture, supported by the guarantee. It was held that the guarantee was effective, because there had been an estoppel: the bank had relied on the statement about execution, and had changed its position to its detriment by advancing the money (*TCB Ltd* v *Gray* [1986] Ch 621; issue not decided on appeal).

2 New enduring powers of attorney

(a) Prescribed form

An enduring power of attorney must be in the prescribed form (1985 Act, s 2(1) (*a*)). The form which has been prescribed includes explanatory notes (Prescribed Form Regulations, Schedule; Practice Direction [1989] 2 All ER 64). An instrument differing in an immaterial respect in form or mode of expression is sufficient (s 2(6)).

The present form was prescribed for use from 31 July 1990. For the earlier forms, see below p 51.

The form contains statements intended to draw to the attention of the parties the nature of the power, and the attorney's obligations (1985 Act, s 2(2)(*b*)). Specifically, there is a statement by the donor that he intends the power to continue in spite of his becoming mentally incapable and that he has read, or had read to him, the information explaining the effect of creating the power. It also contains a statement by the attorney that he understands the statutory duty of registration.

When more than one attorney is appointed, the power must make it clear whether they are to act jointly, or jointly and severally (1985 Act, s 11(1)).

(b) Adapting form

Users of the earlier editions of the form encountered difficulties in adapting them to particular cases. In particular, it seemed to be required that an adaptation was made by deleting an irrelevant operative part of the form, but the side note referring to it had to be retained. As a result, there is now express authority (Prescribed form Regulations, reg 2(2), (3)):

  (i) to omit references to a second attorney, and whether the appointment is joint and several where only one attorney is appointed;
 (ii) to use only one of any pair of alternatives;
(iii) to omit the reference to conditions and restrictions on the attorney's authority where there is none;
 (iv) to omit the provision for attestation by a second witness where there is only one;
  (v) to omit any marginal note referring to a provision omitted;
 (vi) to omit the head notes to Part C;
(vii) to allow the donor or an attorney to make his mark instead of signing.

3 Execution

(a) Witnesses

For the valid execution of a deed by an individual at least one witness is essential. The donor must sign the deed (or make his mark on it) in the presence of a witness who attests the signature, or it can be signed on his behalf in his presence and that of two witnesses who attest the signature (Law of Property (Miscellaneous Provisions) Act 1989, s 1(3), (4)). There is no requirement as to the competence or the independence of the witnesses.

(b) Enduring powers of attorney

Exceptionally, detailed provisions are made about witnessing signatures enduring powers of attorney. A witness is required to sign and give his full name and address. It need not be the same witness, and indeed if there is more than one the parties need not execute the document at the same time. The other restrictions are that the donor and an attorney cannot witness each other's signature, and that no attorney may witness another's signature (Prescribed Form Regulations, reg 3). A side note to the prescribed form says that 'it is not advisable' for a married person to witness the signature of his or her spouse. This is not explained, and cannot have any binding force.

The Prescribed Form Regulations' requirements about witnessing are mandatory, so a document not complying with them cannot be a valid enduring power. Queries could however arise with a power appointing joint and several attorneys. Say that three attorneys are appointed, A, B and C, and that A's signature is witnessed by B and B's and C's are witnessed by an independent third party. A's execution is clearly invalid. C's is valid, and the power can take effect in his favour. But does the fact that *B* witnessed *A*'s signature invalidate his own signature? It is suggested that it should not, because his own execution should not be in doubt, but the point has not been settled.

(c) Trustees

A separate statutory provision requires an individual trustee who delegates his functions under the Trustee Act power to have at least one witness attesting his execution of the power of attorney (Trustee Act 1925, s 25(3); 1971 Act, s 9(2)), although this is now effectively subsumed by the general rule for executing deeds.

(d) Companies

A company need no longer have a common seal, and may execute a power of attorney in accordance with the rules governing all deeds. The document must be signed by a director and the secretary or by two directors and be expressed to be executed by the company (Companies Act 1985, s 36A(4); Companies Act 1989, s 130(2)). Companies may still nevertheless use seals.

A power of attorney executed by a company under seal must be witnessed as the articles of association of the company require. Table A prescribed under the Companies Act 1985 requires that an instrument which is sealed be signed by a director and the secretary of the company or by two directors. The directors may vary this (Companies (Tables A to F) Regulations 1985, art 101). Under the Companies Act 1948, the second signatory could be some other person appointed by the directors for the purpose (Table A, art 113).

It is often convenient to take advantage of the provision that, in favour of a purchaser, a deed purporting to be sealed by a company in the presence of and attested by a director and secretary, or other permanent officer or his deputy, is deemed to be duly executed and to take effect accordingly (Law of Property Act 1925, s 74(1)). A similar provision applies where a company executes without a seal (Companies Act 1985, s 36A(6); Companies Act 1989, s 130(2)).

Some foreign companies do not have a seal, because none is required by the law of the country of their incorporation. It seems that until now such a company has been incapable of executing a deed recognised by English law, and therefore it could not grant a power of attorney. In practice, however, a declaration or affidavit confirming the validity under the law of the company's incorporation of the procedure adapted may be accepted. There is power for the Secretary of State to make regulations applying to companies incorporated outside Great Britain the rules for execution without a seal (Companies Act 1989, s 130(6)), but none has yet been made. (See the requirements on claiming money in court, p 68.)

(e) Attorney

Only in the case of an enduring power of attorney is the instrument normally executed by the attorney, and in that case it is mandatory if the power is to survive the donor's mental incapacity. For an ordinary power, such execution would normally be unnecessary and inappropriate, because if the power is a deed poll the attorney is not a party to it.

There will be some cases, particularly on the grant of a power coupled with an interest, where the power is part, and often a subsidiary part, of a contract. In such a case, it is often essential, because of the other contents of the document, that both parties execute it. The fact that even on the grant of a simple power of attorney there may be reciprocal obligations does not mean that the attorney must execute it. The authority is offered to the attorney on conditions, for example, that he exercises it in a certain way, and in return he has the benefit of the donor's covenant to ratify his acts. These conditions are activated upon the attorney exercising the powers granted to him.

An enduring power must be executed by the attorney (1985 Act, s 2(1)(*b*)). Until he has executed it, the power may (if worded appropriately) take effect as an ordinary power, but not an enduring one. If more than one attorney is appointed and they are to act jointly and severally, the power takes effect as an enduring power in favour of those attorneys who have executed (s 11(4)). When attorneys are appointed to act jointly, all must execute before the power is good as an enduring one.

4 Earlier enduring powers of attorney

The current prescribed form of enduring power of attorney is the third edition. Earlier forms will still have to be registered, and it is essential to ensure that the right form was used, because each form was only prescribed for a limited period, although a valid power was not revoked by the introduction of a new form. The periods for using the forms overlapped, and were as follows:

1st edition: 10 March 1986 to 30 June 1988.
2nd edition: 1 November 1987 to 30 July 1991.
3rd edition: 31 July 1990 onwards.

The superseded forms are reproduced in Appendix 2, as part of the relevant statutory instruments, so that older powers can be checked.

5 Stamp duty

(a) Duty abolished

No stamp duty is payable on powers of attorney executed on or after 19 March 1985, and not stamped before 26 March 1985 (Finance Act 1985, s 85, Sch 24, para (g)). Details of the duty previously charged, and the exemptions from the charge, are given below so that the validity of earlier instruments may be assessed.

(d) Duty formerly charged

Stamp duty was charged on powers of attorney under the head, 'Letter or Power of Attorney, and commission, factory, mandate or other instrument in the nature thereof'. Immediately before abolition, the general rate of duty was 50p (Stamp Act 1894, Sch 1). This head covered more than mere powers of attorney. Any written delegation by one person to another to act in the first's name was covered (*Walker* v *Remmett* (1846) 2 CB 850). However, a donor who gave his attorney further instructions did not attract any further duty (*Parker* v *Dubois* (1836) 1 M&W 30).

The fact that a power was granted by more than one donor, or to more than one attorney, did not of itself attract more than one charge to duty. That was so, even though the powers conferred by the document related to more than one matter (Finance Act 1927, s 56).

(c) Reduced rates

Reduced rates of stamp duty were charged on the following powers:

    (i) by any petty officer, seaman, marine, or soldier serving as a marine, or his representatives, for receiving prize money or wages: 5p;

    (ii) for the receipt of the dividends or interest of any stock: where made for the receipt of one payment only: 5p; in any other case 25p;

    (iii) for the receipt of any sum of money, or any bill of exchange or promissory note for any sum not exceeding £20 or periodical payment up to £10 a year (not covered by any earlier charge): 25p.

(d) Exemptions

Certain powers of attorney were exempt from stamp duty. These were in addition to general exemptions from duty:

    (i) letter or power of attorney for the receipt of dividends of any definite or certain share of Government or Parliamentary stocks or funds, producing a yearly dividend of less than £3;

    (ii) letter or power of attorney or proxy filed in the Family Division of the High Court of Justice in England or the Probate Division in Northern Ireland, or in any ecclesiastical court;

    (iii) order, request or direction under hand only from the proprietor of any stock to any company or to any officer of any company or to any banker to pay the dividends or interest arising from the stock to any person therein named;

    (iv) letter or power of attorney for sale, transfer or acceptance of any of the Government or Parliamentary stocks or funds (Finance Act 1917, s 30);

    (v) power of attorney given exclusively for the purpose of authorising the receipt of money payable on the redemption of Government stock (Finance Act 1921, Sch 3, para 4);

    (vi) power of attorney authorising the receipt of any savings bank annuity or any part thereof (Government Annuities Act 1929, s 58; Finance Act 1970);

    (vii) in the case of winding up by the court or of a creditors' voluntary winding up of a company registered in England, every power of attorney, paper proxy, etc, relating solely to the property of any company which was so wound up, or to any proceedings under any such winding up (Companies Act 1948, s 339(1));

    (viii) for the sole purpose of appointing or authorising a proxy to vote at any one meeting at which votes might be given by proxy, whether the number of persons named in the instrument be one or more (Finance Act 1949, s 35, Sch 8, para 18). An instrument of proxy authorising voting at a particular meeting or any further adjournment of it 'or at any new extraordinary general meeting' to deal with stated matters was not exempt (*Marx* v *Estates and General Investments Ltd* [1976] 1 WLR 380);

    (ix) appointment of proxy to vote at a parliamentary or local election (Representation of the People Act 1949, ss 14(6), 25(6)).

Chapter 7

Duration of Power

1 Period of authority

The period for which authority is granted by a power of attorney is of importance to all concerned. For the donor, it defines for how long he has granted the attorney the ability to deal with his property or affairs; it informs the attorney when he will cease to have the right to bind the donor, after which he would lay himself open to claims for breach of warranty of authority; it limits the time during which a third party may safely deal with the attorney as representing the donor. In some circumstances, a third party may be protected when dealing with the attorney even though the power is no longer valid (see Chapter 12, p 82).

A power may come to an end by effluxion of time, by operation of law, by the donor revoking it, or by the attorney releasing or disclaiming it. Some powers are irrevocable, or may only be revoked by the donor with the attorney's consent. They may in fact come to an end, but they could theoretically be permanent.

2 Termination by effluxion of time

(a) Specified period

A power of attorney may be expressed to be granted for a stated period. When that period comes to an end, the power expires without further formality. A prime example of this type of power is one granted by an individual trustee under the Trustee Act which cannot be for longer than twelve months (Trustee Act 1925, s 25(1); 1971 Act, s 9(2)).

In interpreting a power of attorney, 'month' means calendar month (Law of Property Act 1925, s 61), and references to a time of day refer to Greenwich mean time or summer time as the case may be (Interpretation Act 1978, ss 9, 23(3)).

(b) Purpose specified

If a power of attorney is granted to authorise a single act, or in connection with one specified venture, it necessarily comes to an end when that purpose is achieved. This applies to a power granted to allow an attorney to execute a conveyance to complete a specified sale of land. Once the conveyance is executed, the power is spent. Similarly, a power of attorney delegating a partner's powers under a partnership agreement comes to an end if the partnership is dissolved.

(c) Until incapacity

Because of the statutory authority to exercise trust powers conferred on attorneys under enduring powers (1985 Act, s 3(3)), there may be people who wish to create an enduring power but to limit its operation to the period during which they remain mentally capable. The same might also be the case, although less compellingly, on account of the statutory powers to confer benefits and make gifts (s 3(4),(5)).

There seems no reason in principle why such a limit should not be imposed on an enduring power of attorney. Indeed, there is a case for saying that the authority to exercise trust powers to sell land cannot survive mental incapacity (p 33). However, the effect of the 1985 Act's provision that 'the power shall not be revoked by any subsequent mental incapacity' (s 1(1)(a)) must be considered. This could be read as invalidating any provision ending the authority given by the power at that point. This does not seem a likely interpretation. The words make it clear that an enduring power survives incapacity, which an ordinary power does not. If a power contains an express term limiting its effectiveness to the donor's period of capacity, it is not the incapacity that cancels the authority, but the power itself.

Nevertheless, a valid enduring power must contain a statement by the donor 'that he intends the power to continue in spite of any supervening mental incapacity of his' (1985 Act, s 2(2)(b)(ii)). The power will therefore necessarily appear contradictory on its face, if it also contains a clause which brings it to an end in that contingency.

(d) Future period

A power of attorney need not be granted to take effect immediately. It may come into force on a future date specified in the document. Or, it may be triggered by a future event, for example when the donor leaves the country. In the case of an enduring power, it could commence on the donor becoming incapable (although there is probably a better way to achieve this effect: pp 119–120). The only requirement is that the time the power becomes effective can be identified with certainty.

3 Termination by operation of law

(a) Want of capacity

If the donor ceases to have the capacity to do the acts for which a power of attorney delegates authority, that power comes to an end by operation of law. To this common law rule there is a major exception: an enduring power of attorney is not revoked by the donor's mental incapacity (1985 Act s 1(1)(a)). There are other exceptions in the case of irrevocable powers coupled with an interest. Subject to those exceptions, such disabilities as the death, dissolution or mental incapacity of the donor terminate the attorney's authority. The disability does this automatically, and it makes no difference that the attorney is unaware of what has happened (*Yonge* v *Toynbee* [1910] 1 KB 215). However, the attorney incurs no liability if he acts under the power in ignorance of its revocation (1971, Act, s 5(1)).

(b) Destruction of subject matter

Some earlier editions of this book suggested that the destruction of the subject matter of a power of attorney brought the power to an end. Although it would clearly render the power ineffective, there seems no ground to suppose that it would actually be terminated. This distinction might be important if after the destruction there was a reconstruction or the donor acquired something else to which the power could be construed to refer.

4 Revocation

(a) Consent of attorney

Normally the revocation of a power of attorney is a unilateral act by the donor. Just as he does not need the attorney's consent to grant the power, he does not need that consent to end it. However, the attorney's consent may be made a condition precedent to the revocation of a power coupled with an interest in circumstances in which it can be irrevocable. A power given as security, stated to be irrevocable and protected by statute, can only be revoked with the attorney's consent.

The donor may contract that he will not revoke the power for a particular period. That would be unusual. It may be that in other cases where the power of attorney is part of a commercial relationship, and 'especially those involving mutual trust and confidence', the donor is only entitled to revoke it where it is reasonable to do so (*Martin-Baker Aircraft Co Ltd* v *Canadian Flight Equipment Ltd* [1955] 2 QB 556). Nevertheless, a donor can revoke a power in defiance of such restraints. That may render him liable to damages, but the power is effectively revoked.

(b) Express revocation

An express revocation of a power of attorney should be by deed. A precedent is set out in Appendix 3. After an enduring power of attorney has been registered, there are formalities to be completed before any revocation can be valid.

If the donor considers that there is a danger that the attorney will continue to act under the power of attorney notwithstanding its revocation, thereby continuing to bind him opposite third parties, he should take all the steps he can to ensure that the revocation comes to the attention of third parties. There is no prescribed general way to notify them.

Where the danger concerns a limited number of third parties—eg, the donor's bank—the surest course is to notify each of them individually. Some earlier editions of this book recommended endorsing a memorandum of the notification on the power of attorney. This presupposes that it is in the hands of the donor, which is unlikely. However, now that the contents of a power can be proved by the production of a photocopy, an endorsement would be no guarantee against misuse: a copy made earlier, before the memorandum was on it, could be used.

(c) Implied revocation

If the donor of a power of attorney does an act which is incompatible with the continued operation of the power, it is revoked. An enduring power cannot, however, be revoked by implication once it is registered. An example of implied revocation is provided by a shareholder who appoints a proxy for attending a particular meeting. He revokes the instrument of proxy by attending in person and voting (*Cousins* v *International Brick Co Ltd* [1931] 2 Ch 90). Suitably drawn articles of association for the company concerned could reverse that effect.

There are few cases in which such an act by the grantor will be unequivocal. The authority that a power of attorney grants is normally concurrent with that of the donor. The fact that the donor himself does something that the attorney could have done under the power does not, therefore, prejudice the power. A power of attorney allowing the attorney to draw cheques on the donor's bank account may, for example, result in both the donor and the attorney drawing on the account.

It is unwise for a donor to rely upon an implied revocation. It should be confirmed by an express revocation without delay. An attorney who comes to hear of an act on the donor's part that might be construed as an implied revocation should immediately ask the donor for clarification of the position.

(d) Enduring powers of attorney

Once an enduring power of attorney has been registered, the donor cannot revoke it unless and until the Court of Protection confirms the revocation (1985 Act, s 7(1)(a)). The court must be satisfied on two points. First, the donor must have done all that was necessary in law to effect an express revocation. Secondly, the donor must have been mentally capable of revoking the power at the time he did so, whether or not he is still capable when the court considers the application. If those two points are established, the court is obliged to confirm the revocation (s 8(3)).

5 Irrevocable powers

(a) At common law

A power of attorney coupled with an interest is irrevocable at common law while that interest subsists (*Walsh* v *Whitcomb* (1797) 2 Esp 565). This applies to a power given to a creditor to sell land and to retain the proceeds to repay himself (*Gaussen* v *Morton* [1830] 10 B&C 731). A power linked to a mortgage remains irrevocable until the money has been repaid (*Barclays Bank Ltd* v *Bird* [1954] Ch 274).

A distinction must be drawn between a power coupled with an interest, and a case in which the interest is only collateral to the power. The latter does not render the power irrevocable (*Chinnock* v *Sainsbury* (1860) 30 LJ Ch 409). An example of a collateral interest is a solicitor's lien for his costs over the deeds of property in respect of which his client has given him a power of attorney.

(b) Powers given as security

Section 4 of the 1971 Act gives express statutory power to make powers of attorney given as security irrevocable. This overlaps with the common law power. The powers to which this applies are those given to secure either a proprietary interest of the attorney, or the performance of an obligation owed to the attorney. This definition seems to make the class coextensive with powers coupled with an interest. In addition, the power must be expressed to be irrevocable.

The section does not require that the power be given for valuable consideration, as did earlier provisions now repealed (Law of Property Act 1925, s 126(1)). Giving sufficient consideration has sometimes been equated with coupling an interest with a power. 'What is meant by an authority coupled with an interest being irrevocable is this,—that where an agreement is entered into on a sufficient consideration, whereby an authority is given for the purpose of securing some benefit to the donee of the authority, such an authority is irrevocable' (*Clarke* v *Laurie* (1857) 2 H&N 199, 200 per Williams J).

The attorney must have a proprietary interest, or some obligation must be owed to him. A company which gave a power of attorney to a receiver under a debenture did not create a power given as security, because that requirement was not satisfied (*Barrows* v *Chief Land Registrar* [1977] CLY 315).

This is the effect of the section on a power that qualifies. So long as the attorney has the proprietary interest, or the obligation to him remains undischarged, the power cannot be revoked by the donor unilaterally. Nor do the death, incapacity or bankruptcy of the donor affect it. Similarly, a power granted by a corporation is not revoked by the donor's being wound up (*Sowman* v *David Samuel Trust Ltd* [1978] 1 WLR 22), or dissolved.

This provision applies to powers whenever they were created (1971 Act, s 4(3)). The earlier statutory provisions are explained in connection with dealings with land (pp 99–100).

(c) Other powers expressed as irrevocable

The 1971 Act tackles the problem that a third party dealing with an attorney appointed by a power purporting to be given as security and expressed to be irrevocable cannot know whether it does truly come into the category dealt with in the last section. It does so by giving the third party equivalent protection, while not making the power irrevocable.

If on the face of it a power is expressed to be given as security and to be irrevocable, a third party who does not know that it was not in fact given as security can assume that it is only revocable with the attorney's consent (1971 Act, s 5(3)).

As between the donor and the attorney, such a power is not irrevocable. An attorney who continues to purport to exercise his authority once it has been revoked runs the risk of liability to the donor for any loss he causes.

The problems arising in earlier powers of attorney which were expressed to be irrevocable are dealt with in relation to dealings with land, because their importance in practice is now mostly confined to powers forming part of the title to land.

6 Disclaimer

(a) General

The attorney may renounce or disclaim the authority which a power of attorney grants to him. This ends the authority (Law of Property Act 1925, s 156(1)). The renunciation should be communicated to the donor, who is then entitled to rely on the attorney not exercising the authority.

A precedent for a formal deed of disclaimer is included in Appendix 3.

(b) Enduring powers of attorney

Special rules apply to the disclaimer of enduring powers of attorney, because they are intended to make permanent provision for the management of the donor's affairs, and if the attorney disclaims it may be necessary to make alternative arrangements. With an ordinary power, the validity of the disclaimer is often not important, because an attorney who does not wish to take action under the authority the power confers can simply refrain from doing anything. In the case of an enduring power, however, the attorney has a statutory duty to apply to register it when the donor is becoming, or has become, mentally incapable, and an effective disclaimer is the only way in which he can escape liability.

What must be done by an attorney seeking to disclaim depends upon whether or not the donor is still mentally capable. While he is, notice of the disclaimer must be given to the donor, and it is not valid until this is done (1985 Act, s 2(12)). Once the attorney has reason to believe that the donor is, or is becoming, incapable, or if the power has actually been registered, the attorney must give notice of the disclaimer to the Court of Protection on form EP3. The disclaimer is effective once that notice has been given (ss 4(6), 7(1)(b)) which means the day on which the court receives the notice (Court Rules, r 9(8)).

A precedent for a notice of disclaimer is included in Appendix 3.

7 Presumption of nonrevocation

In certain circumstances, there is a presumption in favour of a purchaser that a third party dealing with an attorney had no knowledge of any revocation of the power. This makes the transaction with the attorney as valid as if the power were still subsisting. See p 84.

Chapter 8

Exercising a Power

1 Using donor's name

It is generally advisable and convenient for an attorney to exercise the powers granted to him in the donor's name. If he contracts in his own name, and he can generally choose that alternative, the third party with whom he is dealing will not be put on notice that the attorney is contracting on the donor's behalf. The attorney then runs the risk of incurring personal liability.

An attorney has express statutory power to execute instruments with his own name. He may do any other thing in his own name. This is as effective as if the instrument was executed or the act done in the donor's name (1971 Act, s 7(1)).

The normal form of execution of a deed by an attorney is:

'AB [donor]

by his attorney

CD [attorney]'

An alternative is:

'CD [attorney]

as attorney for and on behalf of

AB [donor]'

Where there are joint attorneys, both should sign, but no particular wording is required, other than referring to 'attorneys' in the plural. Where more than one attorney is appointed to act jointly or severally, one or more of them can sign, but no reference to the position is needed on the face of the document.

2 Powers granted by corporations

An attorney acting under a power granted by a corporation may act in his own name or in the corporation's name, as is the case with powers granted by other donors (1971 Act, s 7(1),(2)). There are special statutory provisions covering this case, which may be used as an alternative.

A conveyance of property in the name of the corporation (including a corporation sole) may be signed by the attorney in the name of the corporation in the presence of at least one witness (Law of Property Act 1925, s 74(3); Law of Property (Miscellaneous Provisions) Act 1989, Sch 2). In this context, 'conveyance' includes a mortgage, charge, lease or any other assurance of property, which would include a Land Registry transfer (s 205(1)(ii)).

Execution of a deed under this provision would be in this form:

'SIGNED ON BEHALF OF   XYZ Limited [donor]
XYZ LIMITED FOR   by its attorney
DELIVERY AS A DEED in
the presence of: AB [attorney]'
  CD [witness]

A similar, but not identical, provision applies to an attorney appointed by a registered company to execute deeds outside the United Kingdom (Companies Act 1985, s 38; Companies Act 1989, Sch 17, para 7).

In this case the attorney must 'execute' the deed, rather than merely signing it. The following form should be used:

'SIGNED AS A DEED AND
DELIVERED BY AB [attorney]   AB'
ON BEHALF OF XYZ LIMITED
in the presence of:
  CD [witness]

Alternatively, a company which has a common seal may have a facsimile of it—called an official seal—for use outside the United Kingdom. The seal has on the face of it the name of every territory, district or place where it is to be used. The company may empower attorneys to affix that seal. That authority need not itself be under seal. It would be necessary expressly to authorise sealing officers if no directors were available overseas for that purpose. To verify the validity of a sealing under this provision, the person affixing the seal must certify on the deed the date and place at which the seal is affixed (1985 Act, s 39; 1989 Act, Sch 17, para 2). The following is a form of execution which complies with these provisions:

'THE OFFICIAL SEAL OF XYZ LIMITED was
hereunto affixed in the presence of AB and

CD (duly authorised in that behalf by an
instrument under the common seal of XYZ   Official
Limited dated the   day of   19)   seal'
at   on the   day of   19
as the said AB and the said CD
hereby certify:
   AB
   CD

3 Corporation as attorney

Where a corporation is appointed attorney, it may execute deeds on
the donor's behalf under its own common seal (or by the signatures of
a director and the secretary or two directors: Companies Act 1985,
s 36A(4); Companies Act 1989, s 130(2)) as attorney. This procedure
will often be inconvenient, and an alternative is provided by statute.
The board of directors, council or other governing body of the
corporation may, by resolution or otherwise, appoint someone to
execute deeds and other instruments in the donor's name. An
instrument that appears to be executed by an officer so appointed is
deemed, in favour of a purchaser, to have been executed by an officer
who was duly authorised (Law of Property Act 1925, s 74(4)).
'Purchaser' here means a purchaser in good faith for valuable
consideration and it includes a lessee and a mortgagee (s 205(1)(xxi)).
It is therefore useful for the document to show the officer's authority
on the face of it. The testimonium could read:

'IN WITNESS whereof AB [the officer] an officer of XYZ
Limited [the attorney] duly appointed by the board of directors
of XYZ Limited by resolution dated the   day of
19   to execute deeds in the name of CD [donor] in
exercise of the power in that behalf granted by CD to XYZ
Limited by a Power of Attorney dated the   day of
     19   has hereunto set the hand of CD the day and
year first before written.'

The deed would then be executed:
'CD [donor]
by authority of his attorney XYZ Limited
AB [officer]'

The statutory procedure for delegation to an officer of the attorney
corporation applies equally if the donor, as well as the attorney, is a
corporation.

The memorandum and articles of association of a company acting as an attorney, or the charter or other governing instrument of a corporation, may lay down some other way for it to delegate the execution of documents on the donor's behalf. The general statutory provisions do not supersede any such other arrangements (Law of Property Act 1925, s 74(6)).

4 Bills of exchange

A power of attorney may authorise the drawing, accepting and endorsing bills of exchange and promissory notes on the donor's behalf. A registered company may authorise any person to sign bills and notes on its behalf (Companies Act 1985, s 37).

The donor is expressly protected by statute if the attorney makes it clear that he signs on behalf of the donor. 'A signature by procuration operates as notice that the agent has but a limited authority to sign, and the principal is only bound by such signature if the agent in so signing was acting within the actual limits of his authority' (Bills of Exchange Act 1882, s 25). This means 'that a person who takes a bill or note so accepted or indorsed ["per pro"] is bound at his peril to inquire into the extent of the agent's authority' (*Bryant, Powis and Bryant Ltd* v *La Banque du Peuple* [1893] AC 170, 177 per Lord Macnaughten).

For this reason, there is a clear advantage to a donor in requiring, in the power, that the attorney always signs in such cases explicitly on the donor's behalf.

5 Proving authority

(a) Power of attorney

An attorney may establish his authority by producing the original power, but he also has the alternative of doing so by producing a copy.

If a copy is to prove the contents of a power of attorney it must meet the following requirements (1971 Act, s 3(1),(3)):

(1) It must be reproduced photographically or by some other device for reproducing documents in facsimile.

(2) It must bear a certificate at the end that the copy is a true and complete copy of the original. There has been no reported dispute about the positioning of the certificate—unlike the litigation over the positioning of the signature 'at the foot or end' of a will (Wills Act 1837, s 9 (as substituted by the Administration of Justice Act 1982,

s 17))—but it should be noted that a copy certified in any other position does not satisfy the statutory condition.

(3) If the original consists of two or more pages, it must bear a certificate at the end of each page to the effect that it is a true and complete copy of the corresponding page of the original. This precludes copying a power of attorney in such a way that there is a change in pagination, either by reproducing more than one page of the original on one page of the copy or by showing only part of an original page on a sheet of copy.

(4) Every certificate must be signed by a solicitor, notary public or by a stockbroker who is a member of any stock exchange within the meaning of the Stock Transfer Act 1963 or the Stock Transfer Act (Northern Ireland) 1963.

As well as a copy of the original, the contents of a power of attorney may be proved by a copy of a copy, which itself satisfies the four conditions set out above. In that case, the copy of the copy must also comply with the conditions, but the certificates will refer to the first copy instead of to the original.

These provisions were novel when introduced by the 1971 Act. They replaced the former practice of filing powers in the central office of the Supreme Court, which enabled office copies to be obtained to prove the contents of the power when it was necessary to produce proof to a number of people simultaneously. The old provisions are dealt with in Chapter 14 (p 95), as they may still be of importance in matters of title.

Two points should be noted. First, the provisions about facsimile copies apply equally to powers created before 1 October 1971, when the 1971 Act came into force. Secondly, it is still possible to bespeak office copies of some powers filed while that facility remained available.

(b) Registration of power

Once an enduring power of attorney has been registered, an office copy of it issued out of the Court of Protection is evidence in any part of the United Kingdom of the contents of the instrument, and of the fact that it has been registered (1985 Act, s 7(3)). It is still possible to provide evidence of an enduring power in the same way as for other powers, as explained in the previous paragraph (s 7(4)).

Any person may apply for an office copy of a registered enduring power of attorney, but before issuing it the Court of Protection must be satisfied that he has good reason for requesting a copy and that it is not reasonably practicable for him to obtain one from the attorney

(Court Rules, r 12(2)). Application to the court is on Form EP4, which also requests a search to ascertain whether the power is registered (Sch 1). The fee is £5 (Sch 2).

An office copy of an enduring power of attorney need not contain the explanatory information which constitutes part of the prescribed form (Court Rules, r 12(4)). Its absence from an office copy is therefore no evidence that it was not on the original.

(c) Court of Protection orders

The Court of Protection has a wide jurisdiction in connection with enduring powers of attorney, including their interpretation. If it is necessary to establish the contents of an order of the court, an office copy is admissible in all legal proceedings as evidence of the original (Mental Health Act 1983, s 109(2)).

6 Custody of power

As a power of attorney is the instrument giving an attorney his authority, which he will be called upon to exhibit to those with whom he deals on the donor's behalf, he normally is given custody of it.

Before the enactment of the 1971 Act, a donor who wished to revoke a power gained considerable protection against the unauthorised further exercise of the authority it granted, by retaking custody of the power. At that time, the power's contents had to be proved by production of the original, or of an office copy of it. A formal deed of revocation could be filed in court, which would cause the filed power to be marked as revoked, and prevent the issue of further office copies of an apparently valid power. The donor was at risk from any earlier office copies which were extant, but no further. Now that privately produced copies can prove the contents of a power, or even a copy of a copy, there is little or nothing the donor can do to prevent a fraudulent attorney proliferating them.

In two cases, an enduring power of attorney has to be delivered up to the Court of Protection, unless the court otherwise directs. These are: first, if the court refuses an application to register the power, except on the ground that it is premature because the donor is not yet mentally incapable (1985 Act, s 6(8)); secondly, if the court cancels a registration, except on the ground that the donor is, and is likely to remain, mentally capable (s 8(4)).

7 Legal proceedings

An attorney who sues on behalf of a donor should do so in the donor's name (*Jones and Saldanha* v *Gurney* [1913] WN 72). When the donor is abroad, and indeed that is the reason for granting the power of attorney, the fact that he is the only plaintiff may result in his being ordered to give security for costs.

Where money is to be paid out of court, the Accountant General is bound to act on the request of an attorney to make the payment for the credit of the payee's account in a United Kingdom bank or a bank in the country where the payee resides (Supreme Court Fund Rules 1975, r 39(2)). A power executed by a foreign company should have attached to it an affidavit of verification. This is preferably made by a notary public before a British consular official. It is to establish that the company is duly constituted and registered under the local law of the foreign country; that the signatories to the power are directors and secretary of it, as the case may be; that it has no common seal, if that is the case; and that the signatures of those who signed bind the company.

Chapter 9

Duties of Donor

1 Warranty of ability to delegate

It is for the donor of a power of attorney to establish that he is entitled to grant the power which he purports to do. The attorney is generally entitled to rely on its validity. Circumstances may put an attorney on notice that the power may not or cannot be validly granted. For example, it should be obvious to an individual that he cannot properly be granted authority to deal with trust property by his only cotrustee, unless an enduring power is used.

In normal cases, where there is no reason for the attorney to doubt the power granted to him, he is not bound to make investigations to assure himself that any of his actions under the power will be valid.

The attorney may find himself personally at risk. If the donor has contracted with a third party not to compete in a particular field, an attorney who knows nothing of that restriction may make competitive arrangements on the donor's behalf. The third party could be in a position to seek an injunction to restrain both the donor and his attorney. In such a case, the attorney may seek an indemnity from the donor. He is entitled to damages on breach of what amounts to a warranty that the donor validly granted to the attorney the authority stated in the power of attorney.

2 Indemnity

In addition to cases arising because the donor has empowered the attorney to do more than he was entitled to delegate, the donor is generally liable to indemnify his attorney against expense and liability that he properly incurs in the performance of acts under a power (*Westropp* v *Solomon* (1849) 8 CB 345). This duty does not extend to a case where the attorney exceeds his authority and the act is not ratified by the donor (*Barron* v *Fitzgerald* (1840) 6 Bing NC 201).

69

3 Ratification

Notwithstanding the undertaking on the part of the donor to ratify whatever the donor does, commonly found in ordinary powers of attorney, ratification is rarely appropriate. Ratification is the subsequent validation of an act done by the attorney which was not authorised at the time it was done. It should not be necessary, or indeed possible, in respect of acts done pursuant to the power. As they are authorised at the time they are done, they are immediately valid, and need no ratification. If, on the other hand, an attorney exceeds his powers, his acts do not, in the absence of ostensible authority, bind the donor. The donor is not obliged to ratify such an action, which would involve his widening the scope of the authority that he delegated (*Midland Bank Ltd* v *Reckitt* [1933] AC 1).

In a case where the power is defective, either for some want of formality not apparent on the face of it or because of some collateral arrangement with a third party, there is a duty on the donor to stand behind the attorney and ratify the acts he does which would have been valid and within the power, but for the circumstances of which the attorney was ignorant. In those circumstances, it is considered that the donor has a duty to ratify the attorney's acts—or to put the attorney in the same position as if he had ratified—and that he has that duty whether or not it is expressly stated in the power.

Chapter 10

Duties of Attorney

1 To act within authority

An attorney has a duty to the donor of the power of attorney which appointed him to act only within the limits of the authority conferred by the power. The scope of the attorney's authority may be defined expressly—by the actual words of the power—or impliedly, for example, by circumstances as where the principal object of the power carries with it authority to do necessary ancillary acts.

In the case of an enduring power of attorney which has been registered, this limitation can be overridden by an order of the Court of Protection, which has jurisdiction to give directions as to the management or disposal by the attorney of the property and affairs of the donor (1985 Act, s 8(2)(*b*)(i)). But this is restricted to administrative matters (*Re R (Enduring Power of Attorney)* [1989] 2 WLR 1219).

That jurisdiction can be exercised even before the power is registered, if the court has reason to believe that the donor is becoming, or has become, mentally incapable (s 5). In that case the original power must be submitted (*Practice Direction* (1986) 130 SJ 324). Application to the court is by letter, unless the court otherwise directs, when Form EP3 must be used (Court Rules, r 7(1)). The letter must contain the applicant's name and address and the donor's name, and state the form of relief or determination required and the grounds for the application (r 9(2)).

While the donor of a power may be bound by the acts of an attorney which fall outside his actual authority but come within his ostensible authority, this extension is irrelevant to the relations between a donor and his attorney. 'If the question arises between the principal and the agent—either of them claiming against the other—actual authority must be proved. There is no question of ostensible authority as between those two parties, the principal and the agent' (*Hely-Hutchinson* v *Brayhead Ltd* [1968] 1 QB 549, 593 per Lord Pearson).

However, if an attorney purports to act in his capacity as attorney and in doing so makes a profit, even though acting beyond the scope of his authority, he is bound to account to the donor for the profit (*Reading* v *Attorney-General* [1951] AC 507). This presumably does not apply to the remuneration of a professional attorney (pp 44–45).

It certainly does not apply to an attorney appointed by an enduring power of attorney who exercises his statutory authority to take a benefit, or make a gift in his own favour, from the donor's estate in circumstances in which he is allowed to do so, or under the authority of an order of the Court of Protection (1985 Act, s 3(4),(5),8(2)(*e*); pp 14–15).

Unless the power directs the attorney to carry out authorised acts in a particular way, he is entitled to choose the method to adopt. He must proceed reasonably. He may be guided by custom where it is reasonable, or where it may be assumed that the donor knew of the custom.

If the power of attorney is ambiguous, the attorney is protected while he acts bona fide on a reasonable interpretation of it (*Weigall & Co* v *Runciman & Co* (1916) 115 LT 61).

The question also arises whether the attorney is under an obligation to do what he has authority to do, for instance, is there a positive obligation to act, or merely a negative obligation not to go beyond the scope of the authority if he decides to act at all? There is a distinction to be made here between a gratuitous attorney and an attorney who is paid. An unpaid attorney need not do anything. An attorney for reward has an obligation to carry out any duties that he undertakes, and is liable for nonfeasance.

It follows from the attorney's duty to act within the scope of his authority, that he must also restrict his actions to the period of validity of the power. In general, if he purports to exercise his authority after the power has been revoked, he is liable in damages to compensate the donor for any loss suffered. However, if the attorney did not know of the revocation when he did the act, he incurs no liability (1971 Act, s 5(1)).

2 Standard of care

The standard of care that an attorney must bring to carrying out his duties varies depending whether or not he is paid. If paid, he must exercise the care, skill and diligence of a reasonable man. Further, if he undertakes those duties in the course of a profession, he must exercise proper professional competence. A volunteer attorney must use such skill as he possesses, and show such care and skill as he would display in conducting his own affairs. Here again, even though he is not paid, if the attorney holds himself out as having the necessary skills, he must come up to the standard he has set himself.

3 Good faith and disclosure

The attorney must not put himself in a position where his duty to the donor conflicts with his duty to someone else. There will be cases where the donor is himself aware of a conflict. If he knows before making the appointment, the attorney is not at fault. But once the attorney has accepted the appointment, he must make a full disclosure to the donor before accepting any conflicting employment.

The position of an agent serving two different principals was examined by Donaldson J in *North and South Trust Co* v *Berkeley* [1971] 1 WLR 470, in the context of Lloyd's insurance brokers whose practice was to represent the insured in effecting the policy, and both the insured and the underwriters in negotiating settlement of a claim. He said (p 484), 'Fully informed consent apart, an agent cannot lawfully place himself in a position in which he owes a duty to another which is inconsistent with his duty to his principal.' The principal's consent can be derived from a common usage, but such usage 'must at least be notorious, certain and reasonable' (p 482). An attorney with a conflicting interest is liable to compensate the donor for any resulting loss.

The question arises whether the attorney who is liable in breach of this duty to the donor can validly contract on the donor's behalf and bind him. If the contract is with a third party, the normal principles apply, and the donor is bound to the extent of the attorney's ostensible authority. However, if the contract is made on the donor's behalf with the attorney's second principal, the donor can avoid it. Further, if the second principal knew of the existing relationship between the donor and the attorney, the court will assume that the consideration he gave as his part of the bargain would, but for the arrangement with the attorney, have been greater by the amount of any payment he made to the attorney.

The attorney is under a duty to account to the donor for any profit he makes from a third party. Similarly, the donor has a right to any secret profits or bribes that the attorney receives.

The donor's rights are not all cumulative. Where the attorney is guilty of a fraud that results in the disposal of one of the donor's assets at an undervalue, or the acquisition on his behalf of something at too great a price, and the attorney receives a bribe for his connivance, the donor has a choice. He can either recover damages for fraud—which in this example would be the difference between the price and the value of the asset—or he may require the attorney to account for the bribe. He is not entitled to both. The donor is put to his election, but does not have to choose until the time that judgment is entered in his favour on one of the two causes of action (*Mahesan S/O Thambiah* v *Malaysia Government Officers' Co-operative Housing Society Ltd* [1979] AC 374).

4 Accounting

The attorney has a duty to keep the donor's money separate from his own, and from any other people's that he has in his hands. Complying with accounting requirements such as those imposed on solicitors for clients' money generally is presumed to satisfy this requirement, without the need to keep the money in a separate bank account. The attorney's duty extends to keeping up-to-date records of the state of account between the two parties. If the donor entrusts his books to his attorney, they must be produced to the donor on demand.

The attorney holds the donor's money as trustee (*Burdick* v *Garrick* (1870) LR 5 Ch App 233: money paid by a solicitor attorney into his firm's account, before professional accounting rules were imposed). The trust stems from the obligation to keep the money apart. 'It is clear that if the terms upon which the person receives the money are that he is bound to keep it separate, either in a bank or elsewhere, and to hand that money so kept as a separate fund to a person entitled to it, then he is a trustee of that money and must hand it over to the person who is his cestui que trust' (*Henry* v *Hammond* [1913] 2 KB 515,521 per Channell J). The trust extends to any interest earned by the money. It arises without the donor being informed that the money has been set aside (*Re Chelsea Cloisters Ltd* (1980) 41 P&CR 98).

The result of the money being held on trust is that the statute of limitations does not run against the donor to prevent his claiming the money. It also saves the donor's money from forming part of the attorney's estate if the attorney goes bankrupt.

The Court of Protection can make an order giving directions to an attorney appointed under an enduring power of attorney as to the rendering of accounts and the production of the records he keeps for that purpose (1985 Act, s 8(2)(*b*)(ii)). Application to the court is by letter, unless the court requires the use of Form EP3 (Court Rules, r 7(1)). The letter must contain the applicant's name and address and the donor's name, and state the form of relief or determination required and the grounds for the application (r 9(2)).

5 Personal performance

An attorney is only entitled to delegate his powers and duties where he has authority to do so, whether expressly or by implication. There is an implied power to delegate purely ministerial acts. In other cases, the position has been summed up in this way, 'an authority . . . may and should be implied where, from the conduct of the parties to the original contract of agency, the usage of trade, or the nature of the particular business which is the subject of the agency, it may reasonably be presumed that the parties to the contract of agency originally intended that such authority should exist, or where, in the course of employment, unforeseen emergencies arise which impose upon the agent the necessity of employing a substitute' (*De Bussche* v *Alt* (1878) 8 ChD 286, 310 per Thesiger LJ).

An enduring power of attorney cannot authorise the attorney to appoint a substitute (1985 Act, s 2(9)).

Some of the reasons why an attorney, like any other agent, can only delegate where specially authorised, were illustrated in the case of an estate agent appointed to sell a house. 'The reason is because an estate agent holds a position of discretion and trust. Discretion in his conduct of negotiations. Trust in his handling of affairs . . . Furthermore, he is at liberty in the course of the negotiations to receive a deposit as stakeholder' (*John McCann & Co* v *Pow* [1974] 1 WLR 1643, 1647 per Lord Denning MR).

Generally, there is no contract between the donor of a power and his attorney's substitute. They will not therefore be able to sue each other for breach of contract, but in an appropriate case the donor would be able to take action in tort.

Nevertheless, it is possible for the donor to give the attorney power to delegate and to create privity of contract between the donor and the substitute. This would be unusual. It requires that the donor contemplated that certain acts would be done by a substitute, and that he gave the attorney power to create privity of contract between him and the substitute (*Calico Printers' Association* v *Barclays Bank Ltd* (1931) 145 LT 51, 55).

6 Confidentiality

An attorney, like other agents, is under a duty to keep the donor's affairs confidential, unless the donor authorises him to disclose them (*LS Harris Trustees Ltd* v *Power Packing Services (Hermit Road) Ltd* [1970] 2 Ll Rep 65). He is also limited in the extent to which he is entitled to use the knowledge he acquires as attorney. He may not put what he learns in the course of his duties to his private benefit, nor may he solicit the donor's customers (*Julien Praet et Cie SA* v *HG Poland Ltd* [1962] 1 Ll Rep 566).

These duties continue after the power comes to an end (*Amber Size and Chemical Co Ltd* v *Menzel* [1913] 2 Ch 239).

7 Registration of enduring power

The attorney under an enduring power of attorney has a duty to apply to the Court of Protection to register the power as soon as practicable when he has reason to believe that the donor is, or is becoming, mentally incapable (1985 Act, s 4(1),(2)). The details are given in Chapter 13, p 89.

8 Court of Protection jurisdiction

The Court of Protection has an extensive jurisdiction over attorneys appointed under enduring powers of attorney which have been registered, and this includes imposing duties on the attorneys (1985 Act, s 8(1)). Even before registration, these powers can be exercised if the court has reason to believe that the donor is becoming, or has become, mentally incapable (s 5).

The court has powers (1985 Act, s 8(2)(*b*)–(*g*)):

(i) to give directions as to the management or disposal by the attorney of the donor's property and affairs;

(ii) to direct the rendering of accounts by the attorney, and the production of the records he keeps for that purpose;

(iii) to give directions regarding the attorney's remuneration or expenses, whether or not they are mentioned in the instrument, including the power to make orders to repay excessive remuneration, or to pay additional sums;

(iv) to require that the attorney furnish information or produce documents or things which he has in his possession in his capacity as attorney;

(v) to give any consent or authority which the attorney would have had to obtain from a mentally capable donor;

(vi) to authorise the attorney to benefit himself, or persons other than the donor, in some way beyond the general statutory authority.

An application to the court is by letter, unless it otherwise directs, when Form EP3 must be used (Court Rules, r 7(1)). The letter must contain the applicant's name and address and the donor's name and state the form of relief or determination required and the grounds for the application (r 9(2)). An application before the power is registered must be accompanied by the original power (*Practice Direction* (1986) 130 SJ 324).

Chapter 11

Protection of Attorney

1 General

An attorney who purports to act under a power of attorney which is invalid—either because it was not validly granted, so that it never conferred any authority, or because it has ceased to be valid, either through expiry or revocation—can be liable for any loss which his act causes to others. In the absence of statutory intervention, there are three possible types of claim he may face. First, the donor of the power may claim for the wrongful disposal of his property, or other loss caused by unauthorised interference in his affairs. Secondly, a person with whom the attorney contracts, purportedly on behalf of the donor, will have a claim for breach of warranty of authority. Thirdly, there could also be a claim from a third party more remotely affected, for instance, taking property from the person who bought from the attorney, and finding himself without proper title.

If the attorney is aware that his authority under the power of attorney is at an end, but nevertheless continues to act under the power, he is justifiably liable.

However, if the power is revoked without his knowledge, he can find himself unwittingly liable. It is possible for the donor to revoke a power of attorney without notifying the attorney. Further, and probably more seriously, there are cases in which the law impliedly revokes a power. The moment the donor dies, any power he granted ceases to have effect. An ordinary power, although not an enduring power, is revoked when the donor ceases to have mental capacity. Not only is that revocation automatic, but it is frequently impossible to say precisely when it takes effect.

Statute has recognised the difficulty in which these rules may place an honest attorney, and has provided protection. An attorney who acts in pursuance of a power when it has been revoked incurs no liability provided he did not at the time know that it had been revoked (1971 Act, s 5(1)). Certain points should be noted. First, the attorney must act 'in pursuance of the power', which means that his act must be one which, had the power still been in force, it would have authorised. No protection is afforded to an attorney doing an act for which he would not have had authority in the first place, or continuing to act after a time limit expressly imposed by the original instrument. Secondly, the attorney is protected against liability both to the donor and to others. Thirdly, knowledge of the revocation removes the protection. It does not matter from what source he learns that the power has been revoked. However, in the case of an enduring power, when a donor's revocation of a power has to be confirmed by the Court of Protection—which is after the power has been registered— the attorney is deemed to know that the power has been revoked if he knows of the court's confirmation, but not if he merely knows of the unconfirmed revocation (1985 Act, s 9(5)).

2 Purported enduring powers of attorney

There is a special statutory protection for an attorney appointed by an instrument in the proper form for an enduring power of attorney, but which is not valid as an enduring power, ie it creates an ordinary power. It applies whether or not the power has been registered (1985 Act, Sch 2, para 1). The protection applies when the power has been revoked by the donor's mental incapacity. The attorney who acts in pursuance of the power incurs no liability, whether to the donor or anyone else. To this there is one exception. There is no protection for an attorney who knows both that the instrument did not create a valid power and that the donor was mentally incapable (Sch 2, para 2).

This additional protection is needed because an attorney who believes he is acting under a valid enduring power would justifiably continue to act even though, to his knowledge, the donor had become mentally incapable, subject only to the attorney's obligation to register the power. However, the knowledge of the donor's incapacity would prevent his relying on the general protection for attorneys.

3 Registered enduring powers of attorney

If an instrument which did not create a valid power of attorney is registered as an enduring power, there is automatic protection for the attorney, even if the registration has been cancelled at the relevant time. It should be noted that the provision applies to an instrument which did not create a valid power, rather than merely one which did not create a valid *enduring* power (but see below).

The benefit which the attorney enjoys is that if he acts in pursuance of the power, he incurs no liability, either to the donor or to any other person, by reason of the nonexistence of the power (1985 Act, s 9(1)). To this there are three express exceptions, when the protection does not apply:

(1) When the attorney knows that the instrument did not create a valid enduring power. It is not clear what knowledge of the law is to be attributed to the attorney. For example, an instrument which contains a power for him to appoint a substitute or successor cannot create an enduring power. If, by ignorance and oversight, it is registered, is knowledge of the invalidity to be attributed to the attorney?

(2) When the attorney knows that an event has occurred which, had the instrument created a valid enduring power, would have revoked it. The donor's death would be such an event.

(3) When the attorney knows that, had the instrument created a valid enduring power, it would already have expired.

4 Retrospective protection

When an enduring power of attorney has been registered, the Court of Protection has jurisdiction to relieve the attorney wholly or partly of any liability he may have incurred on account of a breach of his duties as attorney (1985 Act, s 8(2)(*f*)). The protection can extend to acts done, or omitted, before the power was, or should have been, registered. It is not necessary to be able to point to specific failure, as relief can be requested from a potential liability. The court can also exercise this jurisdiction before the power is registered, if it has reason to believe that the donor is becoming, or has become, mentally incapable (s 5).

5 Protection in the power

The donor of a power of attorney can expressly relieve the attorney from liability to him in all or specific circumstances. Clearly, if the instrument contains a provision to that effect, the donor would be estopped from taking any action. However, it is doubtful whether the donor could relieve the attorney for the consequences of the attorney's acts after the donor's death (when the property would no longer be his) and it seems unlikely that the donor could effectively protect the attorney from actions by third parties.

6 Limitation period

There is no period of limitation which runs in favour of an attorney to prevent the donor taking action against him for misuse of his authority. This is because, although the attorney is not truly a trustee, he is nevertheless in a fiduciary position (*Burdick* v *Garrick* (1870) LR 5 Ch App 233).

Chapter 12

Position of Third Parties

1 Subsistence of power

A third party dealing with an attorney must, in order to ensure that any contract he negotiates with the attorney binds the donor of the power, assure himself of two things. First, he must be satisfied that the power is still in force. Secondly, he must ascertain that the attorney is acting within the scope of his authority.

Statutory presumptions for the benefit of third parties and purchasers discussed below apply to acts and transactions after 1 October 1971. The date on which the power of attorney was granted is immaterial (1971 Act, s 5(7)).

(a) Power revoked: general

Even if a power of attorney has in fact been brought to an end by revocation, a third party may deal with the attorney in ignorance of the revocation. In such a case, in favour of the third party, the transaction is as valid as if the power were still in existence (1971 Act, s 5(2)). That does not excuse the third party from investigating to make sure that the power was granted in proper form, that there were no circumstances preventing the donor from validly granting a power, and that the transaction falls within the scope of the attorney's authority. The statutory protection simply amounts to the fact that the revocation by itself makes no difference to the position of a third party who knew nothing about it.

A third party who knows of some fact that has the effect of revoking the power, such as the donor's death, knows of the revocation for this purpose and therefore loses the statutory protection (1971 Act, s 5(5)).

It is suggested that this provision should be interpreted to mean that protection extends to a third party who did not know, and *should not have known*, of the revocation, for example, a third party who did not make any enquiries that in the circumstances would have been reasonable, should be treated as knowing what those enquiries would have revealed to him.

(b) Purported enduring powers of attorney

A third party is specially protected if he deals with an attorney under a power which is in the form of an enduring power, whether or not it is registered, but which only creates an ordinary power, when the power has been revoked by the donor's mental incapacity. Any transaction is, in the third party's favour, as valid as it would have been had the power been valid. The only exception to this is when the third party knew both that the instrument did not create a valid enduring power, and that the donor was mentally incapable (1985 Act, Sch 2, paras 1,3).

(c) Registered invalid powers

Someone who deals with an attorney under an instrument which did not create a valid power of attorney, but was nevertheless registered as an enduring power, is protected, even if the registration has subsequently been cancelled. Any transaction is, in favour of the third party, as valid as if the power had been in existence (1985 Act, s 9(3)). There are three exceptions. A person is not protected if he knows:

   (i) that the instrument did not create a valid enduring power;
   (ii) that an event has occurred which, even if it had been a valid enduring power, would have had the effect of revoking it; or
   (iii) that, even if it had been a valid enduring power, it would already have expired.

(d) Power coupled with an interest

A power coupled with an interest, or, as the 1971 Act terms it, a power given by way of security, is in a special position. If the instrument creating it states that the power is to be irrevocable, a third party is entitled to assume that it can only be revoked by the donor with the attorney's consent. The only exception to this is if the third party knows that the power was not in fact given by way of security.

A third party dealing with an attorney under this form of power has the protection of one who does not know of the revocation, unless he knows that it was revoked by the donor with the attorney's consent (1971 Act, s 5(3)). Knowledge of a purported unilateral revocation by the donor does not remove the third party's protection.

(e) Protection of purchasers

Purchasers are protected by special provisions which reinforce the presumption of validity in favour of third parties. They apply where a purchaser's interest depends on the validity of the transaction between the attorney and the third party, and where the appropriate procedure has been followed. For this purpose, 'purchaser' means a purchaser in good faith for valuable consideration. It includes a lessee, mortgagee, chargee by way of legal mortgage, or other person who for valuable consideration acquires an interest in property. 'Purchase' has a corresponding meaning (Law of Property Act 1925, s 205(1)(xxi); 1971 Act, s 5(6); 1985 Act, s 9(7)).

There are two statutory provisions giving protection to purchasers. One, originally designed for ordinary powers of attorney, now applies to all powers. The other is confined to registered enduring powers. In each case there is a conclusive presumption. The general presumption is that the person dealing with the attorney did not at the material time know of the revocation of the power (1971 Act, s 5(4)). In the case of a registered enduring power, it is presumed that the transaction is valid (1985 Act, s 9(4)).

For either presumption to apply one of two conditions must be fulfilled (1971 Act, s 5(4); 1985 Act, s 9(4)):

(1) Either, there is a twelve months' time limit within which the transaction between the attorney and the third party must have taken place. For the general presumption the twelve months runs from the date on which the power came into operation. In the case of a registered enduring power, it runs from the date of registration.

(2) Or, the third party must make a statutory declaration no later than three months after the purchase (ie, the dealing between the third party and the purchaser, not the transaction to which the attorney was a party). In the general case, the declaration is that the third party did not, at the material time, know of the revocation of the power. Where there is a registered enduring power, the declaration states that at the time of the transaction the third party had no reason to doubt that the attorney had authority to dispose of the property in question.

Although the declaration can be made any length of time after the transaction between the attorney and the third party, it is desirable to make it as soon as possible, because if the third party should die there is no one else who can make the declaration in his stead in order to take advantage of the statutory presumption. Precedents for statutory declarations are included in Appendix 3.

(f) Stock exchange transactions

Special statutory protection is conferred in the case of the transfer of a registered security for the purpose of a stock exchange transaction.

2 Scope of attorney's authority

A transaction between an attorney and a third party can only bind the donor of a power of attorney if it is within the attorney's authority. This is something that the third party has to investigate. The donor will not only be bound by an act within the attorney's actual authority, but also by one within his ostensible authority.

(a) Actual authority

The scope of the actual authority of an attorney is dealt with in Chapter 2. Normally, it will be defined by the power of attorney. It can be extended by the donor by a direct communication from him to a third party (*Reckitt* v *Barnett, Pembroke and Slater Ltd* [1929] AC 176: the donor wrote to his bank extending the attorney's authority to draw cheques on his account). The attorney's actual authority can also be restricted by a private communication. If it is only the attorney who is notified, his authority is cut down, but third parties who know nothing of the restriction will probably not be prejudiced because the attorney's ostensible authority will be unimpaired.

(b) Statutory authority: enduring powers of attorney

The grant of an enduring power of attorney confers certain powers on the attorney by statute, unless the instrument itself negatives or restricts the authority. In summary, what the attorney is entitled to do is:

    (i) exercise the donor's powers as trustee (1985 Act, s 3(3); pp 31–32);

    (ii) provide for his own and others' needs to the extent that the donor might have been expected to (s 3(4); pp 14–15);

    (iii) make certain gifts to those (including the attorney) related to or connected with the donor and to charity (s 3(5)).

(c) Ostensible authority

The ostensible authority of an attorney is the authority with which the donor appears to have invested him. The extent of that authority may be judged from the wording of the power, if the third party does not know that it has been modified by some collateral instruction, from general custom or from a course of dealings between the parties in question.

A third party is entitled to rely upon the attorney's ostensible authority even though he did not know when contracting that the attorney was not acting as a principal (*Watteau* v *Fenwick* [1893] 1 QB 346).

A third party is also deemed to know of a limit on the attorney's power of which he was given the opportunity to learn, even though he did not avail himself of that chance (*Jacobs* v *Morris* [1902] 1 Ch 816: the attorney misrepresented his power to borrow; he produced the power of attorney from which the position would have been clear, but the third party did not read it). In the case of bills of exchange, statutory force is given to this rule that a third party is deemed to know the limits of an agent's actual authority if he has notice that the ostensible authority may be circumscribed. 'A signature by procuration operates as notice that the agent has but a limited authority to sign, and the principal is only bound by such signature if the agent in so signing was acting within the actual limits of his authority' (Bills of Exchange Act 1882, s 25).

However, if 'an agent is clothed with ostensible authority no private instructions prevent his acts within the scope of the authority from binding his principal' (*National Bolivian Navigation Co* v *Wilson* (1880) 5 App Cas 176, 209 per Lord Blackburn). This applies even if the possibility that the donor may give the attorney private instructions appears on the face of the power (*Davy* v *Waller* (1899) 81 LT 107).

A restriction on an attorney's authority may be conveyed directly to the third party, or it may be announced publicly to everyone likely to deal with him (*Overbrooke Estates Ltd* v *Glencombe Properties Ltd* [1974] 1 WLR 1335: auction conditions declared that the auctioneers had no authority to make or give any representation or warranty about the property). The limit on the donor's authority may stem from the donor's power to effect a particular transaction, and this may be a matter of law that third parties are assumed to know if they are aware of the relevant facts. The limits on the powers of a trustee or mortgagee to lease property are examples: the ostensible authority of an attorney appointed by a trustee or mortgagee would not extend further, if it was clear to the third party in what capacity the donor was acting.

Special rules apply to companies registered under the Companies Act 1985 or earlier Acts. The validity of a company's act cannot be called into question on the ground of lack of capacity because of anything in its memorandum of association. In favour of a person dealing with a company in good faith, the powers of the directors to bind and to authorise others to do so the company are deemed to be free of any limit under the company's constitution. Moreover, a third party is not bound to inquire into the company's capacity or any limitation on the directors' powers (Companies Act 1985, ss 35–35B; Companies Act 1989, s 108(1)). Accordingly, a third party dealing with a company's attorney appointed by a power executed by the company—which will naturally involve at least one director signing—will not have to investigate any question of capacity unless he has some outside indication of malpractice by any director involved (which might prevent the third party's acting in good faith).

3 Attorney without authority

A third party may be misled by an attorney into thinking that the attorney has authority. If that causes him loss—because the donor is not bound by the attorney's act—the third party may have an action against the attorney. An attorney who acts under a power that has been revoked without his knowledge does not thereby incur liability (1971 Act, s 5(1)).

An attorney may mislead a third party into thinking that the circumstances exist that are necessary to make a conditional power valid. For example, when granted a power to be exercised only while the donor is abroad, the attorney may assure the third party that the donor is abroad when he is not.

The nature and extent of the attorney's liability in such cases varies according to what the attorney knows of the facts.

(a) Deceit

An attorney who knowingly represents to a third party that he has authority to act when he has not, and thereby causes loss to the third party, is guilty of the tort of deceit (*Polhill* v *Walter* (1832) 3 B&Ad 114).

(b) Warranty of authority

An attorney who innocently acts without authority may be liable to a third party who suffers loss for breach of warranty of authority. The attorney is not, however, liable for breach of a contract made on the donor's behalf. The donor cannot be sued if the attorney has no authority, either actual or ostensible, but neither is the attorney liable, because he contracts on behalf of a named principal (*Smout* v *Ilbery*

(1842) 10 M&W 1). The third party can recover from the attorney, as part of his damages for breach of warranty of authority, any costs thrown away in suing the donor on such a contract (*Godwin* v *Francis* (1870) LR 5 CP 295).

The attorney's liability under the warranty has been defined in this way. 'The obligation arising in such a case is well expressed by saying that a person professing to contract as agent for another, impliedly, if not expressly, undertakes to, or promises, the person who enters into such contract upon the faith of the professed agent being duly authorised, that the authority which he professes to have does in point of fact exist. The fact of entering into the transaction with the professed agent, as such, is good consideration for the promise' (*Collen* v *Wright* (1857) 8 E&B 647, per Willes J).

The attorney's representation carries no responsibility if it is as to a matter of law, for instance, as to the correct interpretation of a document (*Rashdall* v *Ford* (1866) LR 2 Eq 750).

Chapter 13

Registration of Enduring Powers

1 Duty to apply

The attorney under an enduring power of attorney has a duty to apply to the Court of Protection to register the power as soon as practicable when he has reason to believe that the donor is, or is becoming, mentally incapable (1985 Act, s 4(1),(2)). It should be noted that for the duty to arise the attorney does not have to be sure, or have proof, that the donor is actually mentally incapable. Belief of a gradual decline into incapability should be enough.

If there are joint attorneys, all must apply for registration, because they only have authority if they all act, and only by registering do they retain full authority. If there is more than one attorney and they have been appointed to act jointly and severally, not all need apply to register, but only those who do will have power to act.

2 Multiple registrations

The 1985 Act is silent about whether more than one enduring power granted by the same donor may be registered. It seems to assume that there would be only one. However, multiple registrations are not ruled out.

If an enduring power is granted for carrying out a trustee's functions by someone who is trustee of a number of settlements, it is conceivable that it should be limited to some only of those trusts. The trustee may decide to execute enduring powers for all his trusteeships, but may understandably conclude that the appropriate attorney is different in some or all of the cases. He can, and therefore should, execute separate powers for each of those attorneys. On his becoming mentally incapable—and assuming that an enduring power granted by a trustee can then continue, which in some cases is a matter of doubt: p 30—each of those powers should be registered. That would seem not only a possible course, but the proper one.

That completely justifiable situation leads on to the possibility of more than one registrable enduring power for nontrustee purposes. Again, there may be good reasons: one attorney may be appropriate to deal with the family home, another to attend to a substantial portfolio of investments. Two limited enduring powers could be granted and each must be registered. In principle there can be nothing against a donor granting more than one general enduring power of attorney. The effect would not be materially different from a power in favour of more than one attorney, authorising them to act jointly and severally. However, separate documents might be used because the donor decided to appoint a second attorney some time after executing the first document.

3 Preliminary notices

Before applying to register, the attorney has to give preliminary notices of his intention to do so, as the Act requires (1985 Act, s 4(3)). Three types of notice may have to given: to the donor, to his relatives and to other attorneys.

Notice of the proposed application must always be given to the donor, unless the attorney has earlier applied to the Court of Protection on Form EP3 accompanied by the original power (Court Rules, r 5(2); *Practice Direction* (1986) 130 SJ 324)), to dispense with the requirement. The application is granted in either of two cases. These are: first, if it would be undesirable or impracticable for the attorney to give him notice; or secondly, if it would serve no useful purpose to do so (1985 Act, Sch 1, paras 3(2), 4).

At least three relatives, if there are three who qualify, must be given notice. The relatives are placed in classes, in an order of priority, and if the requirement to give notice to three relatives means that one in a class is notified, then all in that class must be given notice (1985 Act, Sch 1, para 2(4)). There are some overriding exceptions, when relatives to whom notice would otherwise have to be given do not have to receive it. No notice need be given (Sch 1, paras 2(2), 3(1), 3(2)):

   (i) to a relative whose name and address the attorney does not know and which he cannot reasonably ascertain;
  (ii) to a relative whom the attorney has reason to believe is a minor or is mentally incapable;

(iii) to any attorney under the power who is joining in the application to register;

(iv) in any case in which the Court of Protection has agreed, on the attorney's prior application by letter, that it would be undesirable or impracticable for the attorney to give him notice, or that giving him notice would serve no useful purpose.

The classes of the donor's relatives, in priority order, are (1985 Act, Sch 1, para 2(1)):

(i) husband or wife;

(ii) children;

(iii) parents;

(iv) brothers and sisters, of whole or half blood;

(v) child's widow or widower;

(vi) grandchildren;

(vii) children of brothers and sisters of whole blood;

(viii) children of brothers and sisters of half blood;

(ix) uncles and aunts of whole blood;

(x) children of uncles and aunts of whole blood.

An illegitimate child is treated as the legitimate child of his father and mother (Sch 1, para 8(1)).

Attorneys appointed with joint and several authority are entitled to receive notice of an application for registration in which they are not joining (1985 Act, Sch 1, para 7). No notice need be given to an attorney whose address is not known to the applicant, and cannot be reasonably ascertained by him, or if the applicant has reason to believe that he is a minor or mentally incapable. The applicant may also have the notice requirement waived by the Court of Protection on the grounds either that it would be undesirable or impracticable for notice to be given, or that it would serve no useful purpose.

4 Form of preliminary notices

There is a prescribed form of preliminary notice, which must be used (1985 Act, Sch 1, paras 5,6,7(1); Court Rules, Sch 1, Form EP1). It states that the attorney proposes to make an application to the Court of Protection to register the instrument creating the enduring power. It informs the recipient that he may object to the registration within four weeks of his receiving the notice, and it specifies the possible grounds of objection. The notice to the donor informs him that while the power remains registered, any revocation of it by him is only effective when confirmed by the Court of Protection.

A notice served by post is to be regarded as given on the date it is posted (1985 Act, Sch 1, para 8(2)).

5 Registration application

There is a prescribed form for the application to the court for registration, which must be used (1985 Act, s 4(4); Court Rules, Sch 1, Form EP2). It should be taken or sent by post to The Public Trust Office, Protection Division, Enquiries and Acceptance Branch, 24 Kingsway, London WC2B 6JX.

The application must be made within three days after the date on which the last notice of intention to apply was given to the donor, his relatives and co-attorneys, or after leave was given to dispense with notice (Court Rules, r 6).

The court fee on lodging an application for registration is £30 (Court Rules, Sch 2). Cheques should be made payable to 'Public Trust Office'.

It is a criminal offence for an applicant to make a statement which he knows to be false in a material particular. On summary conviction, the penalty is up to six months' imprisonment or a fine up to the statutory maximum, or both. On indictment, the sentence can be imprisonment for up to two years, or a fine, or both (1985 Act, s 4(7)).

6 Registration procedure

The preliminary notices must be given before the registration application proceeds. Nevertheless, the court still has power to waive the requirement. It may do so if satisfied, in respect of every person who should have been served with notice but has not, either that it was undesirable or impracticable to give him notice, or that no useful purpose is likely to be served by doing so (1985 Act, s 6(3)). Application to the court to exercise that power is made by letter, unless the court directs that it be made on Form EP3 (Court Rules, r 7(1)). The letter must contain the applicant's name and address and the donor's name, and state the form of relief or determination required and the grounds of the application (r 9(2)). If an order appointing a receiver under the Mental Health Act 1983 for the donor is still in force, the registration application will be refused unless the court orders otherwise (s 6(2)).

In three cases, registration will be delayed until the court has made any enquiries it thinks appropriate (1985 Act, s 6(4)). These are: first, if notice of objection is received within five weeks of the last date on which a preliminary notice was served; secondly, if no preliminary notice was served; or thirdly, if the court has reason to believe that enquiries may bring to light evidence on which it would be satisfied that one of the grounds of objection was established. If a ground of objection is established, the registration application will be refused. Otherwise, or if none of the three grounds for enquiring into an application exist, the instrument will be registered (s 6(1),(6)).

7 Grounds of objection

The Act specifies five grounds of objection to the registration of an enduring power (1985 Act, s 6(5)). One or more of them if established, will defeat a registration application, but no other grounds of objection are available. The grounds are:

(1) That the power purported to have been created by the instrument was not valid as an enduring power of attorney. This would be the case, eg, if the attorney had not executed it, or if it purported to give the attorney the power to appoint a substitute or successor.

(2) That the power created by the instrument was no longer subsisting. The supervening mental incapacity of the donor does not affect the position, but other grounds, which would have brought an ordinary power of attorney to an end, would suffice.

(3) That the application is premature because the donor is not yet becoming mentally incapable. It is not necessary to prove that the donor is already incapable.

(4) That fraud or undue pressure was used to induce the donor to create the power. This ground of objection presupposes that the power was initially valid.

(5) That, having regard to all the circumstances and in particular the attorney's relationship to or connection with the donor, the attorney is unsuitable to be the donor's attorney. The position is to be judged when the court comes to consider it, so the circumstances may include matters arising after the execution of the power.

If either of the last two grounds of objection are sustained, the court will revoke the power (1985 Act, s 6(7)).

There is no prescribed form for lodging an objection to registration. It must be in writing, and must state (Court Rules, r 8(1)): the objector's name and address; the donor's name and address, unless it is he who is objecting; any relationship to the donor; the attorney's name and address; and the grounds of objection.

An objection which the court receives on or after the date of registration is treated as an application to cancel the registration (Court Rules, r 8(2)).

8 Cancelling registration

At a later date, the Court of Protection can cancel the registration of a registered enduring power. Application to the court is by letter, unless the court directs that it be made on Form EP3. The letter must contain the applicant's name and address and the donor's name, and state the form of relief or determination required and the grounds of the application (Court Rules, rr 7(1), 9(2)). Cancellation can be on one of the following grounds (1985 Act, s 8(4), Sch 3, para 6):

(i) if the court confirms the revocation of the power by the donor, or receives notice of a disclaimer by the attorney, or any joint attorney;

(ii) if it exercises any power under the Mental Health Act 1983, Pt VII, and directs the revocation of the power;

(iii) if it is satisfied that the donor is, and is likely to remain, mentally capable;

(iv) if it is satisfied that the power has expired, or has been revoked by the death or bankruptcy of the donor, or the death, mental incapacity or bankruptcy of the attorney, or its winding up or dissolution if the attorney is a corporation;

(v) if it is satisfied that the power was not a valid and subsisting power when it was registered;

(vi) if it is satisfied that fraud or undue pressure was used to induce the donor to create the power;

(vii) if it is satisfied that, having regard to all the circumstances and in particular the attorney's relationship or connection with the donor, the attorney is unsuitable to be the donor's attorney.

On the cancellation of the registration on either of the last two grounds, the court will order the revocation of the power (1985 Act, s 8(5)).

Chapter 14

Filed Powers

1 Introduction

· Before 1 October 1971 certain powers of attorney had to be filed at the Central Office of the Supreme Court or at the Land Registry. In addition, other powers could be filed at the court voluntarily. The object of filing was to create a permanent record and to facilitate proof of the contents of the power. Office copies of filed powers could be obtained that were equally admissible with the original.

The possibility of filing powers of attorney was withdrawn on 1 October 1971 (1971 Act, s 2(1); repealed, Supreme Court Act 1981, Sch 7). From that date, the revised system of providing the contents of a power by a certified photostat copy superseded proof by production of an office copy.

The former rules about filing powers remain of importance in assessing the validity of powers pursuant to which documents were executed or acts undertaken prior to 1 October 1971, for example, in examining the title to land. Notwithstanding the withdrawal of filing facilities, it is still possible to obtain office copies of some filed powers.

2 Compulsory filing

In certain cases a power of attorney had to be filed if it was to be valid.

(a) Land

A power authorising the attorney to dispose of or deal with any interest in or charge on land had to be filed. As an alternative, a certified copy of all the relevant portions of it had to be filed (Law of Property Act 1925, s 125(1)). To this, there were three exceptions:

(i) if the power related to a single transaction and the original was handed over on completion;

95

(ii) if the power related only to registered land or a registered charge and, as an alternative, was filed at HM Land Registry;

(iii) if the power of attorney was executed before 1 January 1926 (Law of Property Act 1925, s 125(3)).

A power granted by a trustee who was going to be absent from the United Kingdom might give power to deal with registered land. In that case, the power had first to be filed at the court, and then an office copy had to be filed at HM Land Registry (Trustee Act 1925, s 25(6)).

(b) Trustees

A power of attorney executed by a trustee who intended to remain out of the United Kingdom for over a month, and which delegated any of the trustee's trusts, powers and discretions, had to be filed at the court within ten days after its execution. When filed, it had to be accompanied by a statutory declaration by the donor that he intended to remain abroad for more than a month from the date of the declaration or from a date stated in it (Trustee Act 1925, s 25(4)). For this purpose, the term 'trustee' included a tenant for life and a statutory owner (s 25(11)).

(c) Servicemen

Powers of attorney executed between 12 June 1940 and 31 July 1953 by members of the armed forces outside the United Kingdom, and those executed by British subjects in enemy occupied territory, had to be filed (Evidence and Powers of Attorney Act 1940, s 3).

3 Proof of filed powers

(a) Central Office

Office copies of powers of attorney filed in the Central Office of the Supreme Court after 1967 may still be obtained from the Central Office. Those filed between 1942 and 1967 have been destroyed. Older ones were transferred to the Public Record Office (see below). An office copy is proof of the contents of the power and of the fact that it has been filed, and is admissible in evidence (Supreme Court Act 1981, s 134).

Anyone may search the alphabetical index of donors' names in Room 81 in the Royal Courts of Justice, Strand, London WC2A 2LL, and may inspect any filed instrument or copy. Office copies may be obtained (RSC Ord 63, r 8).

(b) Public Record Office

Powers of attorney filed at the Central Office of the Supreme Court before 1942 are now housed at the Public Record Office, and may be inspected at the Public Record Office, Chancery Lane, London WC2A 1LR. Advance notice should be given. A certified copy under the seal of the Public Record Office is admissible in evidence (Public Records Act 1958, s 9).

(c) Land Registry

A power of attorney, of which the original or a copy is filed at HM Land Registry, is available for inspection to the registered proprietor of the land in respect of which it is filed, or to the proprietor of a charge registered thereon, or to someone authorised by him (Land Registration Act 1925, s 112).

Office copies are generally only issued of documents both filed in the registry and referred to on the register as being filed. A power of attorney would not normally be referred to on the register. If an office copy is made, it is admissible in evidence to the same extent as the original (Land Registration Act 1925, s 113).

4 Filing deeds of revocation

A deed revoking a power of attorney could also be filed at the Central Office of the Supreme Court. If the power had been filed, it was marked 'revoked'. It was not, of course, possible to ensure that office copies issued earlier were so endorsed.

It is still possible to file a deed of revocation.

Chapter 15

Land

1 Unregistered land

(a) Title

A power of attorney forms part of the title to unregistered land when any abstracted document was executed by an attorney. In order to be sure that the document had the effect claimed for it, the validity of the power at the date it was used must be established. The title to land is defective if one of the deeds which goes to make it up was executed under a power of attorney invalid for the purpose (*Walia* v *Michael Naughton Ltd* [1985] 1 WLR 1115).

The power must therefore be abstracted. This applies even if the power was granted before the execution of the root of title, which will necessarily be the case if the document constituting the root of title was itself executed by an attorney (Law of Property Act 1925, s 45(1)). It also applies even if that instrument is the root of title as it is more than 15 years old (*Re Copelin's Contract* [1937] 4 All ER 447). If the power was one that should have been filed at the Central Office of the Supreme Court the abstract should provide evidence that it was indeed filed. A statement in a power granted during the period from 12 June 1940 to 31 July 1953 to the effect that the Evidence and Powers of Attorney Act 1940 did not apply can be relied upon by a purchaser (s 3(3)).

A purchaser of any interest in or charge upon land is entitled to have any power of attorney executed after 1 January 1926 and affecting his title, or a copy of all or the material portions of it, delivered to him free of expense (Law of Property Act 1925, s 125(2)). This right applies equally to a lessee or mortgagee (s 205(1)(xxi)). It cannot be excluded by any contract to the contrary, nor can a contract be rescinded merely because of the enforcement of this right to a copy (s 125(3)).

(b) Pre-1971 Act irrevocable powers

Before the 1971 Act came into force on 1 October 1971, there were other statutory provisions for creating irrevocable powers of attorney after 31 December 1882, on which it may be necessary to rely in making title to unregistered land. There were two categories of irrevocable powers.

First, a power of attorney given for valuable consideration could be expressed to be irrevocable (Law of Property Act 1925, s 126). Secondly, a power could be expressed to be irrevocable for a fixed term of up to one year (s 127).

In either case, this had three effects, either permanently in the case of powers in the first category, or, for those in the second category, during the period for which it was expressed to be irrevocable. In favour of a bona fide purchaser for value, lessee or mortgagee:

- (i) the power was not revoked by the death, disability or bankruptcy of the donor, or by any act of the donor without the attorney's concurrence;
- (ii) any act of the attorney was as valid as it would have been ignoring any of those events in (i) which did not revoke the power; and
- (iii) neither the attorney, nor the purchaser, lessee or mortgagee, was prejudiced by notice of any of the events in (i) declared not to revoke the power.

Questions arose as to the extent to which these powers could be relied upon. It was suggested, for example, that an attorney could not continue to act under the authority conferred by the power after he knew of the donor's death. Also, it was not clear how far a conveyance by the attorney could be effective where the death of the donor had vested the legal estate in his personal representatives.

Nevertheless, it was not the practice to query the execution of an instrument during the period for which a power was expressed to be irrevocable, in the absence of unusual circumstances putting the purchaser on enquiry. Considering the period that must now necessarily have elapsed since a power of attorney was exercised in reliance on these provisions, it is suggested that the grounds for reversing the presumption *omnia praesumuntur solemniter ac rite esse acta* would have to be all the stronger.

Once a period of irrevocability expired, the power did not become void. It continued as a revocable one. In that case, or if there had been no period of irrevocability, the attorney could make a statutory declaration that he had not received any notice or information of the revocation of the power by death or otherwise. A declaration made immediately before or within three months after an act performed under the power was conclusive proof of nonrevocation at the time the act was done (Law of Property Act 1925, s 124(2)).

(c) Waiver of defect

If a seller of land knows of a defect in title relating to a power of attorney, he can by contract oblige the buyer to accept the title as it is, except that he cannot exclude the buyer's right to the delivery of any relevant power of attorney (Law of Property Act 1925, s 125(2)). In the case of a power that is irretrievably lost, the solution appears to be to formulate a contract condition that the seller will make title without reliance upon the instrument executed under the power, even if that means offering a purely possessory title.

In other cases, the buyer can be required to accept a title that is less than perfect as long as he is not misled. Appropriate special conditions might read:

Period of irrevocability expired

'A conveyance of the property agreed to be sold dated   and made between   was executed on behalf of the vendor thereunder by an attorney appointed under a power of attorney dated   which was expressed to be irrevocable for the period of one year from the date of its execution. Notwithstanding that the conveyance was executed more than one year after the power of attorney was granted the Buyer shall assume without requisition or objection that the power of attorney was valid and had not been revoked when the conveyance was executed. The Seller has no evidence that the power of attorney had then been revoked.'

Validity of conditional power

'A conveyance of the property agreed to be sold dated   and made between   was executed on behalf of the vendor thereunder by an attorney appointed under a power of attorney dated   which was expressed to be valid during such time as the vendor was out of the United Kingdom. The conveyance contains a recital to the effect that at the date it was executed the grantor of the power was outside the United Kingdom. The Seller has no reason to doubt the correctness of that recital. The Buyer shall assume it to be a fact and shall not be entitled to raise any requisition thereon nor objection thereto.'

2 Registered land

(a) Procedure

When an instrument delivered to the Registrar in connection with a registration application is executed under the authority of a power of attorney, the original power, a copy of it admissible in evidence or, in the case of a registered enduring power, an office copy must be delivered with it. If the Court of Protection has made an order relating to a registered enduring power or the donor or the attorney (under the 1985 Act, s 8), the order, an office copy of it or a copy certified by a solicitor must be furnished to the Registrar. The Registrar has power to retain the power of attorney, order or the copy, and generally does.

The rules relating to powers of attorney are set out in Land Registration Rules 1925, r 82, as substituted by Land Registry (Powers of Attorney) Rules 1986, r 2.

(b) Proof of nonrevocation

The Registrar will normally only require proof that the power of attorney has not been revoked where the transaction effected by the attorney was not completed within twelve months of the power's coming into operation. The fact that the application to register was later is irrelevant.

The rules lay down the form of statutory declaration that will normally be required to establish nonrevocation in cases where the twelve month period has elapsed. The Registrar can, however, direct that the evidence be in a different form.

In the case of a power in the prescribed form for enduring powers, the person dealing with the attorney must make a declaration. This must deal with three points, relating to his knowledge at the date of completion: first, that he knew of no revocation of the power, whether by the donor or by an order of the Court of Protection; secondly, that he knew of no event which had the effect of revoking the power, for instance, the death or bankruptcy of the donor, the bankruptcy of an attorney or a direction by the Court of Protection exercising its powers under the Mental Health Act 1983, Pt VII; thirdly, that he did not know that the power was invalid as an enduring power and that it had been revoked by the donor's mental incapacity.

Where an ordinary power is not given by way of security, the person dealing with the attorney must make the declaration to say that he did not at the time of completion know of the revocation of the power nor of the occurrence of any event, such as the donor's death, bankruptcy or other incapacity, which would have that effect. If the power is expressed to be irrevocable and to be given by way of security, the declaration must cover two points. The declarant must state that at the time of completion of the transaction he did not know, first that the power was not in fact given by way of security, and secondly that the power had been revoked by the donor with the attorney's consent.

Forms of statutory declaration are included in Appendix 3.

(c) Special cases

It may not be necessary to produce a copy of the power of attorney on each occasion that an instrument executed pursuant to it is presented for registration, in cases where a series of similar transactions is foreseen. It may be possible to lodge one copy on deposit, quoting a deposit number so that the registry may refer to it when dealing with each application.

The Registrar is also prepared to consider making special arrangements, which might be appropriate where a power of attorney is used regularly as a matter of policy over a period that is likely to extend beyond twelve months. Before a person dealing with an attorney relies on such an arrangement—under which the registry agrees to dispense with the statutory declaration that would otherwise be necessary after the power of attorney has been in existence for a year—he should satisfy himself as to the precise terms of the dispensation. It is appropriate to require production of a copy of the registry's letter setting out the terms of the arrangement, and it may be a condition of the arrangement that this is produced.

3 Jointly owned land

Where the legal estate in land, other than settled land, is in joint ownership, the joint owners hold it on trust for sale (Settled Land Act 1925, s 36(1)). Whether or not the legal owners are merely holding on trust for themselves, they are trustees. Accordingly, the 1971 Act form of general power of attorney cannot be used (*Walia* v *Michael Naughton Ltd* [1985] 1 WLR 1115).

There are now two alternatives open to a joint owner who wishes to grant a power of attorney to deal with his interest. He may, first, exercise his right to grant a power under the Trustee Act. This has a number of disadvantages: there is a limit on the period for which the power can be granted; it cannot be granted to the donor's sole cotrustee unless it is a trust corporation; and notice must be given to the other trustees. The alternative course is to grant an enduring power of attorney, which is not subject to these restrictions (1985 Act, s 3(3)). Although the general purpose of an enduring power is to ensure that the donor's mental incapacity does not revoke it (s 1(1)(*a*)), it probably becomes invalid in this type of case because there is duty to discharge or otherwise replace him as trustee (Law of Property Act 1925, s 22(2)). There is consequently some risk to a purchaser in accepting a power of attorney in the enduring form in these circumstances. This can be reduced, although not eliminated, by requiring a statutory declaration by the attorney that the donor is not mentally incapable.

Precedents of a power of attorney for one spouse to grant to the other to sell the jointly owned matrimonial home and of a statutory declaration that the donor has not become mentally incapable are included in Appendix 3.

Chapter 16

Grants of Representation

1 Grant to attorney

(a) Ordinary powers of attorney

An executor or a person entitled to be appointed administrator may appoint an attorney by an ordinary power to apply for letters of administration for his use and benefit. The grant is limited until further representation is granted, or in any other way the registrar directs (Non Contentious Probate Rules 1987, r 31(1)). If the donor is an executor, notice of the application must be given to every other executor, unless the registrar disposes with it (r 31(2)).

An executor who has renounced can apply for a grant as someone else's attorney, but a person who has renounced administration can only do so if a registrar directs (r 37(1),(2)). An attorney's substitute may take a grant if the power gives authority to appoint a substitute (*Palliser* v *Ord* (1724) Bunb 166). Similarly, an attorney's attorney can apply, where the form of delegation is allowed by the law of the deceased's domicile (*In the Goods of Abdul Hamid Bey* (1898) 67 LJP 59).

(b) Enduring powers of attorney

If the donor of an enduring power of attorney is not mentally incapable, the attorney can apply for a grant of representation in the circumstances explained above, as if the power were an ordinary one (Non Contentious Probate Rules 1987, r 31(3)).

Different rules apply in the case of a person entitled to a grant being incapable of managing his affairs by reason of mental incapability. A grant may then be made to an attorney appointed under an enduring power but two conditions must be met. First, all those entitled to a grant in the same degree as the donor must be cleared off, unless a registrar otherwise directs. Secondly, there must be no one authorised to apply by the Court of Protection (r 35(1),(2)).

Notice of an application must be given to the Court of Protection (r 35(5)). The grant is to the attorney for the use and benefit of the donor. It is limited until further representation is granted or in such other way as the registrar directs.

2 Power of attorney

(a) Scope

It must be clear from the power of attorney that it grants authority to the attorney to apply for a grant of administration, normally naming the deceased. A general power is acceptable, particularly in the 1971 Act general form, and may even have been granted before the deceased died (*In the Goods of Barker* [1891] P 251). A power of attorney which only gives authority to administer particular parts of a deceased's estate will not normally be accepted for the purposes of a grant. The authority of a donor and of the attorney should be coextensive.

There is no need for the power to contain any special provisions to enable the attorney to apply for a grant in another estate, to which his position as personal representative in the first one entitles him.

For a precedent of a power of attorney granted by an executor and of a power of attorney granted by a person entitled to letters of administration, see Appendix 3.

(b) Form

Execution of a power of attorney which complies with the 1971 Act satisfies the requirements for appointing an attorney to apply for a grant. The execution should be attested by a disinterested witness. If the donor executes the power in England or Wales before going abroad it should show that he was about to leave. The attorney must swear in his oath that the donor is then residing outside the jurisdiction if that is the case.

Where one attorney is appointed to act on behalf of more than one executor, and the executors live in different countries, there need not be a joint appointment by a single power, although that is acceptable. The alternative is a series of powers in similar terms each making the same appointment on behalf of one of the executors.

Special attention must be paid to the form of the power if it is granted in a country which is not English speaking. When it is written in English it is acceptable if the witness to the donor's signature is a notary or a British consul. In the absence of that attestation, there must be a sufficient indication that the donor understood English.

The extracting solicitor can provide a certificate to that effect. If the power is not in English, a translation certified by a competent authority is required. In cases of doubt whether a country is regarded as English speaking, the question should be referred to a registrar.

(c) Filing

The normal practice is for the power of attorney to be permanently filed in the registry. A general power which is required for other purposes can be issued out again. A copy is lodged with the power and a request for its return. It is then issued with the grant. This arrangement cannot apply to a power that is limited to obtaining the grant.

The power of attorney may have been deposited with a notary or court of law abroad. In such a case, a notarial copy may be filed. It must be accompanied by an affidavit of law that the copy is as valid as the original and would be accepted instead by the court of domicile.

(d) Donor's incapacity

The authority of an attorney under an ordinary power of attorney will come to an end if the grantor becomes mentally incapable before the administration of the deceased's estate has been finished. However, if the donor has appointed the same attorney under an enduring power of attorney with sufficiently wide authority, and that power has been registered with the Court of Protection, the attorney will be able to continue with the administration of the estate.

(e) Donor's death

The donor's death revokes the power of attorney, and therefore the attorney's authority to act in the administration (*Suwerkrop* v *Day* (1838) 8 A&E 624). An attorney who continues to act in ignorance of the donor's death has the general statutory protection. If the administration of the estate is interrupted by the death of the donor, a further grant de bonis non is required.

3 Attorney

(a) Capacity

As the grant of administration will be made to the attorney in his own name, albeit for the use and benefit of the donor, the attorney must have the capacity to take a grant. A minor does not qualify (Non Contentious Probate Rules 1987, r 32). A power of attorney for this purpose may be granted in favour of a member for the time being of a named firm. The attorney's oath must then show that he is a member of the firm.

(b) Responsiblities

An attorney to whom letters of administration are granted is personally fully liable as administrator (*Re Rendell, Wood* v *Rendell* [1901] 1 Ch 230). That liability entitles the attorney to retain the assets while there are outstanding claims against the part of the estate within the jurisdiction, but he must account to his principal for any ascertained surplus. A receipt for that from his principal is a good discharge to the attorney (*Eames* v *Hacon* (1881) 18 ChD 347).

(c) Death

The death of the attorney necessarily brings to an end his power to administer the estate. If the administration is not complete, a cessate grant is needed. The donor may appoint another attorney or may apply for a direct grant.

4 Joint executors

(a) Form of power

Joint executors can all execute one power of attorney appointing a single attorney, or joint attorneys on behalf of them all; or they can execute separate powers, either appointing the same or different attorneys.

If there are more than four executors, and they all execute the same power, it must limit the term of the attorney's appointment. The limitation must be 'until any of us, not exceeding four in number, shall apply . . .'. A power not including that numerical limitation is not acceptable.

(b) Limit on grant

The limit placed on the grant of administration depends on the circumstances.

(1) *Attorney for all executors* The grant is limited until all the executors apply for and obtain probate. If, later, some only of the executors apply, a grant will be made to them if the others have not intermeddled, even through their attorney. If one of the executors dies, the position is uncertain. The grant may cease to be effective. The survivor can revoke the power of attorney, whereupon the court can revoke the grant and issue a fresh one to another attorney appointed under another power (*In the Estate of Dinshaw* [1930] P 180).

(2) *Executors' separate attorneys* The grant ceases on the death of either executor or either attorney. An application for a grant of probate by either executor also brings the attorney grant to an end.

5 Delegation by personal representatives

The power of a personal representative to delegate his function as such after obtaining a grant of representation in his own name is the same as the delegation power of a trustee under the Trustee Act. Presumably an attorney appointed under an enduring power cannot delegate.

Chapter 17

Companies

1 Shareholder's proxy

(a) Right to grant

A proxy is a person appointed by a shareholder of a company to attend and vote at a meeting of the company. Confusingly, the word is also applied to the document granting that authority. The proxy's authority may be general or limited. In the sphere to which his authority relates, a proxy is in effect the shareholder's attorney. He need not himself be a member of the company.

A member of a private company is only entitled to appoint one proxy for any one occasion, unless the articles of the company provide otherwise (Companies Act 1985, s 372(1),(2)).

The right to appoint a proxy applies to members of all companies formed or registered under the Companies Act 1985 and companies existing when that Act was passed (s 735(1)(a)), other than companies without a share capital. In that case, the company's articles can allow the appointment of proxies (s 372(1),(2)).

The appointment of a proxy may be revoked at any time before it is acted upon.

A corporate shareholder has an additional right. It can appoint, by a resolution of the directors or other governing body, a person to attend meetings of any company of which it is a member (s 375(1)). That representative is not a proxy. A proxy's power may be limited, but a corporation's representative is entitled to exercise all the powers that the corporation would have had if it had been an individual shareholder (s 375(2)). He is accordingly counted as one of a quorum (*Re Kelantan Coconut Estates (Ltd and Reduced)* (1920) 64 SJ 700).

(b) Exercising right to appoint

A notice calling a meeting of the members of a company with a share capital must contain a statement, given reasonable prominence, about members' rights to appoint proxies. It must say that a member entitled to attend and vote is entitled to appoint a proxy—or, if allowed, more than one proxy—to attend and vote instead of him. It must add that the proxy need not be a member of the company. It the statement is not included, the officers of the company are guilty of an offence (Companies Act 1985, s 372(3),(4)).

The articles of a company normally require that an instrument appointing a proxy shall be deposited at the registered office of the company, or with its registrar or secretary, prior to the meeting (eg, Companies Act 1948, Table A, art 69; Companies (Tables A to F) Regulations 1985, Table A, art 62). If lodged too late, an appointment is not valid (*Shaw* v *Tati Concessions Ltd* [1913] 1 Ch 292). Any provision requiring an instrument to be lodged more than forty-eight hours before the meeting is void (Companies Act 1985, s 372(5)).

Companies frequently distribute forms for appointing proxies to their members. To do so to only some of the members entitled to be sent notice of a meeting, unless at the written request of a member, is an offence on the part of the officers knowingly and wilfully authorising or permitting it (s 372(6)). Companies whose shares are listed on the Stock Exchange have to undertake to send with a notice convening a meeting two way proxy appointments—ie, forms enabling the shareholder to direct the proxy whom he appoints to vote either for or against, instead of leaving it to the proxy's discretion—for voting on all resolutions intended to be proposed.

(c) Form

A proxy may be appointed generally or for a particular meeting. When appointed in respect of one meeting, the appointment may instruct the proxy how to vote on all or any of the resolutions to be proposed.

The articles of association of a company may prescribe a form of appointment of a proxy (eg, Companies Act 1948, Table A, arts 70, 71; Companies (Tables A to F) Regulations 1985, Table A, arts 60, 61). The Stock Exchange requires that any provision in the articles of a listed company shall not preclude the use of a two way form, and that the articles allow a duly authorised officer of a corporate shareholder to execute a form of proxy under hand.

For examples of instruments appointing a proxy and a resolution appointing a representative, see Appendix 3.

(d) Powers of proxy

A proxy only has an automatic right to speak at a company meeting that he is appointed to attend if the company is a private company

(Companies Act 1985, s 372(1)). Only if the articles of the company allow can a proxy vote on a show of hands (*Bombay-Burmah Trading Corporation* v *Dorabji Cursetji Shroff* [1905] AC 213). A proxy is entitled to demand or join in demanding a poll, by virtue of his authority to vote (s 373(2)).

The proxy's basic right is to vote on a poll. However, if the shareholder who appointed the proxy attends the meeting and votes himself, the proxy's votes will be rejected (*Cousins* v *International Brick Co* [1931] 2 Ch 90). A proxy may be instructed to cast some of the shareholder's votes in one way and some in another. If he casts some of the votes as directed, but withholds the remainder, the votes that he casts are valid (*Oliver* v *Dalgleish* [1963] 1 WLR 1274).

2 Winding up

(a) Proxies

A creditor or contributory may appoint a proxy to attend, speak and vote for him at meetings in the course of a winding up. Some general rules apply to all cases. At any one meeting, only one proxy may actually represent a person entitled to attend, although alternative proxies may be appointed. The chairman of the meeting of the official receiver may be appointed. A proxy must be an adult (Insolvency Rules 1986, r 8.1).

Where the official receiver is appointed, the proxy may be exercised by his deputy, another official receiver or an officer of the Department whom he authorises. A proxy given for a particular meeting extends to adjournments of it (r 8.3).

A proxy may only vote in favour of a resolution which will directly or indirectly result in him, or an associate, receiving remuneration from the insolvent estate if he is specifically directed to do so (r 8.6).

(b) Forms

A series of proxy forms are prescribed by the Insolvency Rules 1986 for use in different cases:

Form 8.1: company or individual voluntary arrangements.
Form 8.2: administration.
Form 8.3: administrative receivership.
Form 8.4: winding up by the court or bankruptcy.
Form 8.5: members' or creditors' voluntary winding up.

When notice is given of a meeting to be held in insolvency proceedings, forms of proxy are sent out with it and no one may be named on it. That form, or one in substantially similar form must be used. It must be signed by the principal, or someone authorised by him stating the nature of his authority (r 8.2).

3 Directors

A director cannot appoint a proxy to act or vote on his behalf as a member of the board. His appointment is personal. The articles of the company may, however, entitle him to appoint an alternate. They should make precise provisions as to the appointment, status and tenure of office of an alternate.

Normally, an alternate is appointed by the director for whom he is a substitute, with the consent of the other directors. The period for which an appointment is made is often limited. While the appointment continues, the alternate exercises the powers, and therefore has the responsibilities, of a director in his own right. His appointment can generally be revoked or suspended by the appointor resuming his duties.

4 Stock exchange transfers

The 1971 Act confers special protection on a person taking a transfer of a registered security when the transfer is executed by an attorney for the purposes of a stock exchange transaction. If the attorney makes a statutory declaration on or within three months of the date of the transfer that the power had not been revoked on that date, there is a conclusive presumption in the transferee's favour that it is so (1971 Act, s 6(1)). This protection is in addition to that provided by s 5, so no declaration is needed when the transfer is made within twelve months of the power coming into operation.

'Registered securities' are transferable securities (shares, stock, debentures, debenture stock, loan stock, bonds, unit trust units, or other securities) whose holders are entered in a register wherever it is maintained. A 'stock exchange transaction' is a sale and purchase of securities in which each party is a member of a stock exchange acting in the ordinary course of his business as such, or is acting through the agency of such a member (Stock Transfer Act 1963, s 4(1); 1971 Act, s 6(2)).

Chapter 18

Using Ordinary Powers of Attorney

Powers of attorney have a very large number of uses by reason of their very adaptability. The following examples are some of those cases where they form an integral part of the documentation for a transaction and which are in common use and of general interest. It is not suggested that these examples are exhaustive, nor even necessarily representative.

1 Purchase of land for resale

A buyer of land who proposes to resell within a reasonably short time can avoid the need, where the title is not registered, to apply for first registration of title and incidentally to pay stamp duty by not taking a conveyance pursuant to his purchase contract. Instead, he is appointed the seller's attorney, and in that capacity executes a conveyance by way of subsale to the eventual buyer. This is particularly suited to a buyer who is going to divide the property and resell the plots, because he avoids awkward Land Registry delays and reduced rates of stamp duty, or even a nil rate, may apply to conveyances of the plots.

The original purchase is completed in all but name, for example, leaving only the execution of the conveyance outstanding, in the usual way. The purchase price is paid to the seller, who hands over the title deeds, thus enabling the buyer freely to make title to subpurchasers.

The buyer should protect the original contract for sale by registration. In the case of land which is already registered, the buyer should consider having the seller's registered address altered to his own.

It is an advantage if the buyer is a company, to avoid complications in making provision in case the buyer dies.

113

The power of attorney can be incorporated into the purchase contract, in which case it must be executed as a deed.

Precedent

(a)   If on completion the Buyer does not take a conveyance/transfer of the property from the Seller the following provisions of this clause take effect

(b)   The Seller irrevocably appoints the Buyer to be his attorney to execute in his name any conveyance/transfer[1] of the legal estate in all or any part of the property sold in favour of the Buyer[2] or any one or more other persons nominated by the Buyer and to acknowledge receipt of all or any part of the purchase money paid hereunder on completion without liability further to account for it to the Seller

(c)   Any conveyance/transfer executed by the Buyer under this power is to be in the form of the draft annexed[3] [mutatis mutandis][4]

(d)   The Seller shall not except at the request of the Buyer grant convey create or dispose of any estate interest or charge in or over the property or any part thereof to any person

---

[1]   The power is deliberately limited to executing conveyances. The drawback of this arrangement is the lack of flexibility for the buyer who cannot eg, mortgage the land for temporary finance, because that would involve imposing repayment or other liabilities on the seller.

[2]   Power to convey to the buyer, rather than to subpurchasers only, allows for a change of plan. The buyer can convey some or all of the property into his own name in order to mortgage it.

[3]   The liabilities that the seller incurs must clearly be limited to those that a normal conveyance pursuant to the contract would have involved, eg, an acknowledgment for production of title deeds and an undertaking for safe custody. Annexing a form of conveyance allows the buyer to demonstrate with certainty to subpurchasers that the authority of the power of attorney extends sufficiently far. An alternative would be for the buyer to covenant to indemnify the seller against the consequences of any provisions in the conveyances that would not normally have appeared, but this is unlikely to commend itself so readily to sellers.

[4]   Some flexibility in the agreed draft is desirable, if only to cope with joint buyers and rights shared between owners of separate plots.

2 Equitable charge over land

An equitable mortgagee of a legal estate in land has the same powers of sale as a mortgagee under a legal mortgage, if the equitable charge is created under seal (Law of Property Act 1925, s 101(1)).

However, it is not clear whether he can, without more, convey the legal estate. Lord Denning MR has argued that he can (*Re White Rose Cottage* [1965] Ch 940), but the safer course seems to be to incorporate a power of attorney into the mortgage to put the matter beyond doubt.

This enables the mortgagee to convey the legal estate, but it is important that it should be conveyed to complete a sale by the mortgagee rather than by the mortgagor. In *Re White Rose Cottage*, the mortgagee executed a transfer in the name of the mortgagor and joined in it in its own name merely to release any mortgagee's claims.

The result was a transfer subject to equities created after the mortgage.

Precedent

The Borrower irrevocably[1] appoints the Lender to be his attorney to [convey] [transfer] the legal estate in fee simple in the property to any person to whom the Lender sells it in exercise of the statutory power of sale freed from all estates interests and rights to which this charge has priority and discharged from any right to redeem this charge.

---

[1] Although expressed to be irrevocable to obtain the advantage of s 5(3) of the 1971 Act, the power will necessarily come to an end on the redemption of the mortgage.

3 Mortgage of flat with tenants' service company

Many schemes for developing blocks of flats, and occasionally other types of property, include provision for each leaseholder of a flat to hold one share in a company which provides the services for the block. Sometimes the company owns the freehold reversion. The intention is that the leases and the shares shall always be owned by the same people. The leases and the articles of association of the company restrict ownership of the one to the person who owns the other.

Difficuities arise when a leaseholder wants to mortgage his lease. The mortgagee must ensure that if he has to exercise his power of sale, not only can he vest the lease in the purchaser, but also the share in the service company. The share itself has little or no intrinsic value, but its ownership is essential to compliance with the tenant's covenants in the lease. The necessary power can be conferred by a clause in the mortgage granting a power of attorney.

Precedent

The Borrower irrevocably[1] appoints the Lender to be his attorney to execute a transfer of the ordinary share of £1 in _____ Limited registered in the name of the Borrower to any person to whom the Lender sells the Property[2].

---

[1] Although expressed to be irrevocable to obtain the advantage of s 5(3) of the 1971 Act, the power will necessarily come to an end on the redemption of the mortgage. Section 6 will not apply, as this share will not be in a quoted company.

[2] It would be more reassuring to the borrower to limit the power by adding the words 'in exercise of the statutory power of sale', but that could involve the company in investigating the nature of the sale of the lease before registering the share transfer. As the sale of the share must necessarily be ancillary to the sale of the flat, this extra safeguard hardly seems necessary.

4 Sale of blocks of flats

When the landlord of a block of flats wants to dispose of his interest he will often have to offer the tenants of the individual flats a statutory right of first refusal (Landlord and Tenant Act 1987, Pt 1). If they pay the same price as the landlord would have obtained elsewhere, which is the intention, it may be thought that he is not prejudiced. But there may be some months of uncertainty before it is clear whether or not the tenants will exercise their rights.

Nothing in the Act precludes a landlord persuading his tenants to contract with him not to exercise their rights. There is a statutory procedure excluding the right of first refusal if a sufficient proportion of tenants notify a prospective purchaser that they will not avail themselves of it (s 18). This does not appear to be available to the landlord in advance of his finding a buyer, but it is suggested that he can legitimately contract to become attorney for the tenants to waive their rights when a prospective buyer serves notices with a view to obtaining waivers.

Precedent

The Tenant irrevocably[1] appoints the Landlord to be his attorney until [date] to receive and respond to any notice served under

---

[1] Although expressed to be irrevocable, the power necessarily expires when the stated period ends.

section 18 of the Landlord and Tenant Act 1987 relating to the sale of [property] for no less than £ [2]

---

[2] Even though the power is given as part of a contract for which the Landlord pays a consideration to the Tenant, it must be a deed to make the power of attorney valid.

5 Share preemption

The articles of association of a private company frequently provide that a shareholder who wishes to sell his shares must first offer them to other members of the company. This is a way to retain within a family the control of a family business, or to restrict the participation of antipathetic people. To ensure that the preemption provisions are promptly complied with, even where the selling shareholder is reluctant, the articles may give the directors power of attorney to execute a transfer of shares. It is not lawful to register a transfer of shares unless a proper instrument of transfer is delivered to the company (Companies Act 1985, s 183(1)). Granting a power of attorney avoids the impasse that could be created if the selling shareholder will not execute a transfer.

Articles of association are not executed as a deed, and indeed may not even have been signed by any of the current members of the company. It is, however, considered that the appointment of an attorney by the articles would comply with the requirements of s 1 of the 1971 Act that 'an instrument creating a power of attorney shall be executed as a deed by . . . the donor'. Nevertheless there is a new doubt. Section 14 of the Companies Act 1985, reads '. . . the memorandum and articles, when registered, bind the company and its members to the same extent as if they respectively had been signed and sealed by each member . . .', and, until 1990, this was assumed to be sufficient. However, that provision has not been amended to accord with the new method for individuals to execute deeds (Law of Property (Miscellaneous Provisions) Act 1989, s 1). The general provision adapting earlier statutory requirements (s 1(7)) does not seem appropriately to cover the position. This doubt remains to be allayed.

Precedent
(a) A member ('transferor') wishing to transfer any shares [otherwise than to another member][1] shall give written notice ('transfer notice'), stating the number of shares and the price of

each, to the Secretary and shall lodge with him the certificate relating to such shares[2]. The Secretary shall thereupon notify the other members of the contents of the transfer notice and the date of its service

(b) Any member ('purchaser') wishing to buy all or any of the shares referred to in the transfer notice shall give notice ('purchase notice') to the Secretary within twenty-eight days of the service of the transfer notice, stating how many such shares he wishes to buy

(c) The transferor shall sell to each purchaser who shall buy the number of shares stated in his purchase notice. If the total number of shares stated in all the purchase notices exceeds the number stated in the transfer notice, the number sold to each purchaser shall be abated rateably

(d) The price for the sale of the shares shall be as stated in the transfer notice unless the purchaser within forty-two days of the service of the transfer notice requests the auditors acting as experts to determine the price, in which event the price shall be as so determined

(e) The sale and purchase of the shares under the terms of this article shall be completed within forty-two days of the service of the transfer notice or (if later) within fourteen days of the determination of the price by the auditors

(f) In default the directors shall have the power at the request of the purchaser to appoint, by a deed executed by two of them, an attorney to execute a transfer of the shares into the name of the purchaser upon receipt of the price which the attorney shall pay to the company to hold on trust for the transferor

(g) If no purchase notice is served within twenty-eight days of the service of the transfer notice, or to the extent that the total number of shares stated in all the purchase notices falls short of the number stated in the transfer notice, the transferor shall be free to transfer those shares or the balance of them free from the provisions of this article.

---

[1] Members may be left free to transfer shares to existing members, but if the shareholders wish to be able to maintain their proportional shareholdings, the preemption article should apply to all transfers.

[2] If the share certificate is lodged, difficulties arising from registering a transfer without cancelling the former certificate will be avoided.

Chapter 19

Using Enduring Powers of Attorney

1 Limited to incapacity

The donor of an enduring power of attorney may wish to execute it as a precaution against future mental incapacity, whether occasioned by illness, accident or old age—much as he might make a will—but may not want it to give the attorney any immediate authority. Granting a power of attorney does not deprive the donor of the power to deal with his own property, but will normally give the attorney concurrent authority. All the same, the donor is entitled to reserve full powers exclusively to himself while he is still capable.

The way to fulfil the purpose of a donor who wants the attorney only to act once he, the donor, is incapable is to make the enduring power exercisable only when it has been registered by the Court of Protection. Admittedly, there is power to register when the donor is only becoming incapable, rather than having lost capacity, but there is the safeguard that the attorney must give the donor preliminary notice of the application to register. One of the grounds of objection to a registration application is that it is premature because the donor is not yet becoming mentally capable (1985 Act, s 6(5)(c)), and a registration can be cancelled if the donor is and is likely to remain mentally capable (s 8(4)(c)). Another possible disadvantage in limiting the use of the power to periods while it is registered is to deprive the attorney of his limited powers while the application is pending (s 1(2)).

Even if the power can only be used after registration, it is convenient to make it come into effect immediately, so that no question arises whether it can be registered. Otherwise, it is conceivable that there could be an argument that the power cannot be registered until effective, but is not effective until registered.

Precedent

The Attorney shall only exercise his authority under this power while and so long as this instrument is registered by the Court of Protection under the Enduring Powers of Attorney Act 1985, or any statutory amendment or reenactment for the time being in force.

2 Successors

What may be seen as one of the weaknesses of the enduring powers of attorney scheme is the prohibition on an attorney appointing his successor (1985 Act, s 2(9)). While it is true that this ensures that the attorney is always the donor's personal choice, it does not, unless he chooses to appoint a trust corporation, provide the continuity that a testator can expect when appointing executors. This may be of little consequence if the donor is elderly, but the middle aged may reasonably see executing an enduring power as a prudent precautionary measure. In such circumstances, one may imagine a man appointing his brother or a parent to act as his attorney should the need arise soon, but preferring that one of his children be his attorney if he remains capable until he is elderly.

The Act's prohibition on appointing a successor applies only to the attorney being allowed to do so; the donor can appoint a successor. The original appointment may therefore be limited in time, or the second appointment can be activated by the death of the first attorney. It has to be borne in mind that each attorney must execute the instrument before it is registered. He must be an adult at the time (1985 Act, s 2(7)(*a*)), but there is no requirement that he be an adult when the donor grants the power. A child who is then a minor can execute the power later, but still before the time has come to register it.

One point which is not certain is whether an attorney must be alive at the date the power is executed. If no attorney is then alive, the deed might be held to be void, but there seems no reason why it should be if the first attorney appointed is then of full capacity. The prospect which this opens is of appointing a child not then born. An example of this is given below, but it must be subject to the caution that its validity might not be upheld.

Precedents

I appoint AB of   to be my attorney until the end of the year 2006, and from the beginning of the year 2007 I appoint CD of   to be my attorney.

I appoint AB of   to be my attorney and upon his
death or his becoming incapable or unwilling[1] to act as my
attorney I appoint CD of   to be my attorney in his
stead.

I appoint AB of   to be my attorney and upon his
death or his becoming incapable or unwilling[1] to act as my attorney
I appoint to be my attorney in his stead any child of mine who has
executed this instrument as attorney (if more than one such
children to act jointly and severally).[2]

---

[1] It would provide useful evidence if the attorney were required to
disclaim formally, by executing a deed of disclaimer, but an attorney
who had shown his unwillingness by neglecting the donor's affairs might
not readily execute such a deed.

[2] If there can be more than one attorney, it is essential to specify whether
they are to act jointly or jointly and serverally (1985 Act, s 11(1)).

3 Joint home ownership

Enduring powers of attorney now offer a way to avoid the
inconvenience that the joint owner of real property cannot grant an
ordinary power of attorney for dealing with his individual interest
(*Walia* v *Michael Naughton Ltd* [1985] 1 WLR 1115). Typically, this
affects a husband and wife owning a matrimonial home jointly. It is
assumed that the authority given to an attorney under an enduring
power of attorney to exercise the donor's power as trustee (1985 Act,
s 3(3)) extends both to trusts in existence at the date of the power of
attorney and those arising later. The latter is necessary if the authority
is to extend to the execution of a mortgage following a purchase.

Precedent
(a) In respect of any land[1] owned by the donor jointly with the
[attorney][2] [any other persons] to join in any contract for the sale of
all or any part of it and to redeem any mortgage or charge affecting
all or any part of it.
(b) [For the purpose of acquiring a home for the donor and his
family][3] to join with the [attorney][2] [wife] [husband] [of the donor]
in purchasing any land, and in charging it by way of [first] legal
mortgage to secure all or part of the purchase price of it.
(c) To sign or execute every contract, document or deed necessary
for any of the foregoing purposes.

[1] The word land is used so that all real property is included, and to avoid trouble about defining what is a house or dwelling.

[2] An enduring power of attorney may validly be granted to the donor's sole cotrustee.

[3] The inclusion of a statement of the reason why the power is granted may cause difficulties, because third parties might require proof of the purpose of a purchase.

Appendix 1

Relevant Acts

Trustee Act 1925, ss 23(2) and 25

Power to employ agents

23.—(2) Trustees or personal representatives may appoint any person to act as their agent or attorney for the purpose of selling, converting, collecting, getting in, and executing and perfecting insurances of, or managing or cultivating, or otherwise administering any property, real or personal, moveable or immoveable, subject to the trust or forming part of the testator's or intestate's estate, in any place outside the United Kingdom or executing or exercising any discretion or trust or power vested in them in relation to any such property, with such ancillary powers, and with and subject to such provisions and restrictions as they may think fit, including a power to appoint substitutes, and shall not, by reason only of their having made such appointment, be responsible for any loss arising thereby.

Power to delegate trusts during absence abroad

25.—[¹(1) Notwithstanding any rule of law or equity to the contrary, a trustee may, by power of attorney, delegate for a period not exceeding twelve months the execution or exercise of all or any of the trusts, powers and discretions vested in him as trustee either alone or jointly with any other person or persons.

(2) The persons who may be donees of a power of attorney under this section include a trust corporation but not (unless a trust corporation) the only other co-trustee of the donor of the power.

(3) Before or within seven days after giving a power of attorney under this section the donor shall give written notice thereof (specifying the date on which the power comes into operation and its duration, the donee of the power, the reason why the power is given and, where some only are delegated, the trusts, powers and discretions delegated) to—

    (*a*) each person (other than himself), if any, who under any instrument creating the trust has power (whether alone or jointly) to appoint a new trustee; and

    (*b*) each of the other trustees, if any;

but failure to comply with this subsection shall not, in favour of a person dealing with the donee of the power, invalidate any act done or instrument executed by the donee.

(5) The donor of a power of attorney given under this section shall be liable for the acts or defaults of the donee in the same manner as if they were the acts or defaults of the donor.]

[²(6) For the purpose of executing or exercising the trusts or powers delegated to him, the donee may exercise any of the powers conferred on the donor as trustee by statute or by the instrument creating the trust, including power, for the purpose of the transfer of any inscribed stock, himself to delegate to an attorney power to transfer but not including the power of delegation conferred by this section.]

[²(7) The fact that it appears from any power of attorney given under this section, or from any evidence required for the purposes of any such power of attorney or otherwise, that in dealing with any stock the donee of the power is acting in the execution of a trust shall not be deemed for any purpose to affect any person in whose books the stock is inscribed or registered with any notice of the trust.]

[³(8) This section applies to a personal representative, tenant for life and statutory owner as it applies to a trustee except that subsection (4) shall apply as if it required the notice there mentioned to be given—

(a) in the case of a personal representative, to each of the other personal representatives, if any, except any executor who has renounced probate;

(b) in the case of a tenant for life, to the trustees of the settlement and to each person, if any, who together with the person giving the notice constitutes the tenant for life;

(c) in the case of a statutory owner, to each of the persons, if any, who together with the person giving the notice constitute the statutory owner and, in the case of a statutory owner by virtue of section 23(1)(a) of the Settled Land Act 1925, to the trustees of the settlement.]

---

1 Section 25(1)–(5) substituted for s 25(1)–(8) by Powers of Attorney Act 1971, s 9(2).

2 Section 25(9),(10) continued in force as s 25(6),(7) by Powers of Attorney Act 1971, s 9(3).

3 Section 25(8) substituted for s 25(11) by Powers of Attorney Act 1971, s 9(3).

Powers of Attorney Act 1971

An Act to make new provision in relation to powers of attorney and the delegation by trustees of their trusts, powers and discretions.

[12th May 1971]

BE IT ENACTED by the Queen's most Excellent Majesty, by and with the advice and consent of the Lords Spiritual and Temporal, and Commons, in this present Parliament assembled and by the authority of the same, as follows:—

Execution of powers of attorney

1.—(1) An instrument creating a power of attorney shall be executed as a deed by the donor of the power.

(2) [*Subsection 2 repealed: Law of Property (Miscellaneous Provisions) Act 1989 ss 1(8), 4, Sch 1, para 6, Sch 2.*]

(3) This section is without prejudice to any requirement in, or having effect under, any other Act as to the witnessing of instruments creating powers of attorney and does not affect the rules relating to the execution of instruments by bodies corporate.

[*Section 2 repealed: Supreme Court Act 1981, Sch 7*]

Proof of instruments creating powers of attorney

3.—(1) The contents of an instrument creating a power of attorney may be proved by means of a copy which—

> (*a*) is a reproduction of the original made with a photographic or other device for reproducing documents in facsimile; and
>
> (*b*) contains the following certificate or certificates signed by the donor of the power or by a solicitor or stockbroker, that is to say—
>> (i) a certificate at the end of the effect that the copy is a true and complete copy of the original; and
>> (ii) if the original consists of two or more pages, a certificate at the end of each page of the copy to the effect that it is a true and complete copy of the corresponding page of the original.

(2) Where a copy of an instrument creating a power of attorney has been made which complies with subsection (1) of this section, the contents of the instrument may also be proved by means of a copy of that copy if the further copy itself complies with that subsection, taking reference in it to the original as references to the copy from which the further copy is made.

(3) In this section 'stockbroker' means a member of any stock exchange within the meaning of Stock Transfer Act 1963 or the Stock Transfer Act (Northern Ireland) 1963.

(4) This section is without prejudice to section 4 of the Evidence and Powers of Attorney Act 1940 (proof of deposited instruments by office copy) and to any other method of proof authorised by law.

(5) For the avoidance of doubt, in relation to an instrument made in Scotland the references to a power of attorney in this section and in section 4 of the Evidence and Powers of Attorney Act 1940 include references to a factory and commission.

Powers of attorney given as security

4.—(1) Where a power of attorney is expressed to be irrevocable and is given to secure—

- (*a*) a proprietary interest of the donee of the power; or
- (*b*) the performance of an obligation owed to the donee, then, so long as the donee has that interest or the obligation remains undischarged, the power shall not be revoked—
  - (i) by the donor without the consent of the donee; or
  - (ii) by the death, incapacity or bankruptcy of the donor or, if the donor is a body corporate, by its winding up or dissolution.

(2) A power of attorney given to secure a proprietary interest may be given to the person entitled to the interest and persons deriving title under him to that interest, and those persons shall be duly constituted donees of the power for all purposes of the power but without prejudice to any right to appoint substitutes given by the power.

(3) This section applies to powers of attorney wherever created.

Protection of donee and third persons where power of attorney is revoked

5.—(1) A donee of a power of attorney who acts in pursuance of the power at a time when it has been revoked shall not, by reason of the revocation, incur any liability (either to the donor or to any other person) if at that time he did not know that the power had been revoked.

(2) Where a power of attorney has been revoked and a person, without knowledge of the revocation, deals with the donee of the power, the transaction between them shall, in favour of that person, be as valid as if the power had then been in existence.

(3) Where the power is expressed in the instrument creating it to be irrevocable and to be given by way of security then, unless the person dealing with the donee knows that it was not in fact given by way of security, he shall be entitled to assume that the power is incapable of revocation except by the donor acting with the consent of the donee and shall accordingly be treated for the purposes of subsection (2) of this section has having knowledge of the revocation only if he knows that it has been revoked in that manner.

(4) Where the interest of a purchaser depends on whether a transaction

between the donee of a power of attorney and another person was valid by virtue of subsection (2) of this section, it shall be conclusively presumed in favour of the purchaser that that person did not at the material time know of the revocation of the power if—

    (*a*) the transaction between the person and the donee was completed within twelve months of the date on which the power came into operation; or

    (*b*) that person makes a statutory declaration, before or within three months after the completion of that purchase, that he did not at the material time know of the revocation of the power.

(5) Without prejudice to subsection (3) of this section, for the purposes of this section knowledge of the revocation of a power of attorney includes knowledge of the occurrence of any event (such as the death of the donor) which has the effect of revoking the power.

- (6) In this section 'purchaser' and 'purchase' have the meanings specified in section 205(1) of the Law of Property Act 1925.

(7) This section applies whenever the power of attorney was created but only to acts and transactions after the commencement of this Act.

Additional protection for transferees under stock exchange transactions

    6.—(1) Without prejudice to section 5 of this Act, where—

    (*a*) the donee of a power of attorney executes, as transferor, an instrument transferring registered securities; and

    (*b*) the instrument is executed for the purposes of a stock exchange transaction,

it shall be conclusively presumed in favour of the transferee that the power had not been revoked at the date of the instrument if a statutory declaration to that effect is made by the donee of the power on or within three months after that date.

(2) In this section 'registered securities' and 'stock exchange transaction' have the same meanings as in the Stock Transfer Act 1963.

Execution of instruments etc by donee of power of attorney

    7.—(1) If the donee of a power of attorney is an individual, he may, if he thinks fit—

    (*a*) execute any instrument with his own signature, and

    (*b*) do any other thing in his own name,

by the authority of the donor of the power; and any document executed or thing done in that manner shall be as effective as if executed or done by the donee with the signature and seal, or, as the case may be, in the name, of the donor of the power.

(2) For the avoidance of doubt it is hereby declared that an instrument to which subsection (3) of section 74 of the Law of Property Act 1925 applies

may be executed either as provided in that subsection or as provided in this section.

(3) This section is without prejudice to any statutory direction requiring an instrument to be executed in the name of an estate owner within the meaning of the said Act of 1925.

(4) This section applies whenever the power of attorney was created.

[*Subsection 8 repealed: Law of Property Act 1925, s 129*]

[*Section 9 amends section 25 of the Trustee Act 1925 which is reproduced on pp 123–4*].

Effect of general power of attorney in specified form

10.—(1) Subject to subsection (2) of this section, a general power of attorney in the form set out in Schedule 1 to this Act, or in a form to the like effect but expressed to be made under this Act, shall operate to confer—

(*a*) on the donee of the power; or

(*b*) if there is more than one donee, on the donees acting jointly or acting jointly or severally, as the case may be,

authority to do on behalf of the donor anything which he can lawfully do by an attorney.

(2) This section does not apply to functions which the donor has as a trustee or personal representative or as a tenant for life or statutory owner within the meaning of the Settled Land Act 1925.

Short title, repeals, consequential amendments, commencement and extent

11.—(1) This Act may be cited as the Powers of Attorney Act 1971.

(2) The enactments specified in Schedule 2 to this Act are hereby repealed to the extent specified in the third column of that Schedule.

(3) In section 125(2) of the Law of Property Act 1925 for the words 'as aforesaid' there shall be substituted the words 'under the Land Registration Act 1925'. [*Words repealed: Supreme Court Act 1981, Sch 7*]

(4) This Act shall come into force on 1st October 1971.

(5) Section 3 of this Act extends to Scotland and Northern Ireland but, save as aforesaid, this Act extends to England and Wales only.

SCHEDULES

Section 10   # SCHEDULE 1
Form of General Power of Attorney for purposes
of Section 10

[This form is reproduced in Appendix 3, Forms of Document, p 194.]

Section 11(2)   # SCHEDULE 2
Repeals

Chapter	Short Title	Extent of Repeal
15 & 16 Geo 5 c 19	The Trustee Act 1925	Section 29
15 & 16 Geo 5 c 20	The Law of Property Act 1925	Sections 123 and 124 Section 125(1) Sections 126 to 129
15 & 16 Geo 5 c 49	The Supreme Court of Judicature (Consolidation) Act 1925	Section 219(1)
4 & 5 Eliz 2 c 46	The Administration of Justice Act 1956	Section 18

Enduring Powers of Attorney
Act 1985

An Act to enable powers of attorney to be created which will survive any subsequent mental incapacity of the donor and to make provision in connection with such powers. [26 June 1985]

BE IT ENACTED by the Queen's most Excellent Majesty, by and with the advice and consent of the Lords Spiritual and Temporal, and Commons, in this present Parliament assembled, and by the authority of the same, as follows:—

Enduring powers of attorney

Enduring power of attorney to survive mental incapacity of donor

1.—(1) Where an individual creates a power of attorney which is an enduring power with the meaning of this Act then—

    (*a*) the power shall not be revoked by any subsequent mental incapacity of his; but

    (*b*) upon such incapacity supervening the donee of the power may not do anything under the authority of the power except as provided by subsection (2) below or as directed or authorised by the court under section 5 unless or, as the case may be, until the instrument creating the power is registered by the court under section 6; and

    (*c*) section 5 of the Powers of Attorney Act 1971 (protection of donee and third persons) so far as applicable shall apply if and so long as paragraph (*b*) above operates to suspend the donee's authority to act under the power as if the power had been revoked by the donor's mental incapacity.

(2) Notwithstanding subsection (1)(*b*) above, where the attorney has made an application for registration of the instrument then, until the application has been initially determined, the attorney may take action under the power—

    (*a*) to maintain the donor or prevent loss to his estate: or

    (*b*) to maintain himself or other persons in so far as section 3(4) permits him to do so.

(3) Where the attorney purports to act as provided by subsection (2) above then, in favour of a person who deals with him without knowledge that the attorney is acting otherwise than in accordance with paragraph (*a*) or (*b*) of that subsection, the transaction between them shall be as valid as if the attorney were acting in accordance with paragraph (*a*) or (*b*).

Characteristics of an enduring power

2.—(1) Subject to subsections (7) to (9) below and section 11, a power of attorney is an enduring power within the meaning of this Act if the instrument which creates the power—

(*a*) is in the prescribed form; and

(*b*) was executed in the prescribed manner by the donor and the attorney; and

(*c*) incorporated at the time of execution by the donor the prescribed explanatory information.

(2) The Lord Chancellor shall make regulations as to the form and execution of instruments creating enduring powers and the regulations shall contain such provisions as appear to him to be appropriate for securing—

(*a*) that no document is used to create an enduring power which does not incorporate such information explaining the general effect of creating or accepting the power as may be prescribed; and

(*b*) that such instruments include statements to the following effect—

(i) by the donor, that he intends the power to continue in spite of any supervening mental incapacity of his;

(ii) by the donor, that he read or had read to him the information explaining the effect of creating the power;

(iii) by the attorney, that he understands the duty of registration imposed by this Act.

(3) Regulations under subsection (2) above—

(*a*) may include different provision for cases where more than one attorney is to be appointed by the instrument than for cases where only one attorney is to be appointed; and

(*b*) may, if they amend or revoke any regulations previously made under that subsection, include saving and transitional provisions.

(4) Regulations under subsection (2) above shall be made by statutory instrument which shall be subject to annulment in pursuance of a resolution of either House of Parliament.

(5) An instrument in the prescribed form purporting to have been executed in the prescribed manner shall be taken, in the absence of evidence to the contrary, to be a document which incorporated at the time of execution by the donor the prescribed explanatory information.

(6) Where an instrument differs in an immaterial respect in form or mode of expression from the prescribed form the instrument shall be treated as sufficient in point of form and expression.

(7) A power of attorney cannot be an enduring power unless, when he executes the instrument creating it, the attorney is—

(a) an individual who has attained eighteen years and is not bankrupt; or

(b) a trust corporation.

(8) A power of attorney under section 25 of the Trustee Act 1925 (power to delegate trusts etc by power of attorney) cannot be an enduring power.

(9) A power of attorney which gives the attorney a right to appoint a substitute or successor cannot be an enduring power.

(10) An enduring power shall be revoked by the bankruptcy of the attorney whatever the circumstances of the bankruptcy.

(11) An enduring power shall be revoked on the exercise by the court of any of its powers under Part VII of the Mental Health Act 1983 if, but only if, the court so directs.

(12) No disclaimer of an enduring power, whether by deed or otherwise, shall be valid unless and until the attorney gives notice of it to the donor or, where section 4(6) or 7(1) applies, to the court.

(13) In this section 'prescribed' means prescribed under subsection (2) above.

Scope of authority etc of attorney under enduring power

3.—(1) An enduring power may confer general authority (as defined in subsection (2) below) on the attorney to act on the donor's behalf in relation to all or a specified part of the property and affairs of the donor or may confer on him authority to do specified things on the donor's behalf and the authority may, in either case, be conferred subject to conditions and restrictions.

(2) Where an instrument is expressed to confer general authority on the attorney it operates to confer, subject to the restriction imposed by subsection (5) below and to any conditions or restrictions contained in the instrument, authority to do on behalf of the donor anything which the donor can lawfully do by an attorney.

(3) Subject to any conditions or restrictions contained in the instrument, an attorney under an enduring power, whether general or limited, may (without obtaining any consent) execute or exercise all or any of the trusts, powers or discretions vested in the donor as trustee and may (without the concurrence of any other person) give a valid receipt for capital or other money paid.

(4) Subject to any conditions or restrictions contained in the instrument, an attorney under an enduring power, whether general or limited, may (without obtaining any consent) act under the power so as to benefit himself or other persons than the donor to the following extent but no further, that is to say—

(a) he may so act in relation to himself or in relation to any other person if the donor might be expected to provide for his or that person's needs respectively; and (*b*) he may do whatever the donor might be expected to do to meet those needs.

(5) Without prejudice to subsection (4) above but subject to any conditions or restrictions contained in the instrument, an attorney under an enduring power, whether general or limited, may (without obtaining any consent) dispose of the property of the donor by way of gift to the following extent but no further, that is to say—

(*a*) he may make gifts of a seasonal nature or at a time, or on an anniversary, of a birth or marriage, to persons (including himself) who are related to or connected with the donor, and

(*b*) he may make gifts to any charity to whom the donor made or might be expected to make gifts,

provided that the value of each such gift is not unreasonable having regard to all the circumstances and in particular the size of the donor's estate.

Action on actual or impending incapacity of donor

Duties of attorney in event or actual or impending incapacity of donor

4.—(1) If the attorney under an enduring power has reason to believe that the donor is or is becoming mentally incapable subsections (2) to (6) below shall apply.

(2) The attorney shall, as soon as practicable, make an application to the court for the registration of the instrument creating the power.

(3) Before making an application for registration the attorney shall comply with the provisions as to notice set out in Schedule 1.

(4) An application for registration shall be made in the prescribed form and shall contain such statements as may be prescribed.

(5) The attorney may, before making an application for the registration of the instrument, refer to the court for its determination any question as to the validity of the power and he shall comply with any direction given to him by the court on that determination.

(6) No disclaimer of the power shall be valid unless and until the attorney gives notice of it to the court.

(7) Any person who, in an application for registration, makes a statement which he knows to be false in a material particular shall be liable—

(*a*) on conviction on indictment, to imprisonment for a term not exceeding two years or to a fine, or both; and

(*b*) on summary conviction, to imprisonment for a term not exceeding six months or to a fine not exceeding the statutory maximum, or both.

(8) In this section and Schedule 1 'prescribed' means prescribed by rules of the court.

Functions of court prior to registration

5. Where the court has reason to believe that the donor of an enduring power may be, or may be becoming, mentally incapable and the court is of the opinion that it is necessary before the instrument creating the power is registered, to exercise any power with respect to the power of attorney or the attorney appointed to act under it which would become exercisable under section 8(2) on its registration, the court may exercise that power under this section and may do so whether the attorney has or has not made an application to the court for the registration of the instrument.

Functions of court on application for registration

6.—(1) In any case where—

    (a) an application for registration is made in accordance with section 4(3) and (4), and

    (b) neither subsection (2) nor subsection (4) below applies, the court shall register the instrument to which the application relates.

(2) Where it appears to the court that there is in force under Part VII of the Mental Health Act 1983 an order appointing a receiver for the donor but the power has not also been revoked then, unless it directs otherwise, the court shall not exercise or further exercise its functions under this section but shall refuse the application for registration.

(3) Where it appears from an application for registration that notice of it has not been given under Schedule 1 to some person entitled to receive it (other than a person in respect of whom the attorney has been dispensed or is otherwise exempt from the requirement to give notice) the court shall direct that the application be treated for the purposes of this Act as having been made in accordance with section 4(3), if the court is satisfied that, as regards each such person—

    (a) it was undesirable or impracticable for the attorney to give him notice; or

    (b) no useful purpose is likely to be served by giving him notice.

(4) If, in the case of an application for registration—

    (a) a valid notice of objection to the registration is received by the court before the expiry of the period of five weeks beginning with the date or, as the case may be, the latest date on which the attorney gave notice to any person under Schedule 1, or

    (b) it appears from the application that there is no one to whom notice has been given under paragraph 1 of that Schedule, or

    (c) the court has reason to believe that appropriate inquiries might bring to light evidence on which the court could be satisfied that one of the grounds of objection set out in subsection (5) below was established, the court shall neither register the instrument nor refuse the application until it has made or caused to be made such inquiries (if any) as it thinks appropriate in the circumstances of the case.

(5) For the purposes of this Act a notice of objection to the registration of an instrument is valid if the objection is made on one or more of the following grounds, namely—

(*a*) that the power purported to have been created by the instrument was not valid as an enduring power of attorney;

(*b*) that the power created by the instrument no longer subsists;

(*c*) that the application is premature because the donor is not yet becoming mentally incapable;

(*d*) that fraud or undue pressure was used to induce the donor to create the power;

(*e*) that, having regard to all the circumstances and in particular the attorney's relationship to or connection with the donor, the attorney is unsuitable to be the donor's attorney.

(6) If, in a case where subsection (4) above applies, any of the grounds of objection in subsection (5) above is established to the satisfaction of the court, the court shall refuse the application but if, in such a case, it is not so satisfied, the court shall register the instrument to which the application relates.

(7) Where the court refuses an application for registration on ground (*d*) or (*e*) in subsection (5) above it shall by order revoke the power created by the instrument.

(8) Where the court refuses an application for registration on any ground other than that specified in subsection (5)(*c*) above the instrument shall be delivered up to be cancelled, unless the court otherwise directs.

Legal position after registration

Effect and proof of registration, etc

7.—(1) The effect of the registration of an instrument under section 6 is that—

(*a*) no revocation of the power by the donor shall be valid unless and until the court confirms the revocation under section 8(3);

(*b*) no disclaimer of the power shall be valid unless and until the attorney gives notice of it to the court;

(*c*) the donor may not extend or restrict the scope of the authority conferred by the instrument and no instruction or consent given by him after registration shall, in the case of a consent, confer any right and, in the case of an instruction, impose or confer any obligation or right on or create any liability of the attorney or other persons having notice of the instruction or consent.

(2) Subsection (1) above applies for so long as the instrument is registered under section 6 whether or not the donor is for the time being mentally incapable.

(3) A document purporting to be an office copy of an instrument registered under this Act or under the Enduring Powers of Attorney (Northern Ireland) Order 1987 shall, in any part of the United Kingdom, be evidence of the contents of the instrument and of the fact that it has been so registered.

(4) Subsection (3) above is without prejudice to section 3 of the Powers of Attorney Act 1971 (proof by certified copies) and to any other method of proof authorised by law.

Functions of court with respect to registered power

8.—(1) Where an instrument has been registered under section 6, the court shall have the following functions with respect to the power and the donor of and the attorney appointed to act under the power.

(2) The court may—

(*a*) determine any question as to the meaning or effect of the instrument;

(*b*) give directions with respect to—
(i) the management or disposal by the attorney of the property and affairs of the donor;
(ii) the rendering of accounts by the attorney and the production of the records kept by him for the purpose;
(iii) the remuneration or expenses of the attorney, whether or not in default of or in accordance with any provision made by the instrument, including directions for the repayment of excessive or the payment of additional remuneration;

(*c*) require the attorney to furnish information or produce documents or things in his possession as attorney;

(*d*) give any consent or authorisation to act which the attorney would have to obtain from a mentally capable donor;

(*e*) authorise the attorney to act so as to benefit himself or other persons than the donor otherwise than in accordance with section 3(4) and (5) (but subject to any conditions or restrictions contained in the instrument);

(*f*) relieve the attorney wholly or partly from any liability which he has or may have incurred on account of a breach of his duties as attorney.

(3) On application made for the purpose by or on behalf of the donor, the court shall confirm the revocation of the power if satisfied that the donor has done whatever is necessary in law to effect an express revocation of the power and was mentally capable of revoking a power of attorney when he did so (whether or not he is so when the court considers the application).

(4) The court shall cancel the registration of an instrument registered under section 6 in any of the following circumstances, that is to say—

(*a*) on confirming the revocation of the power under subsection (3) above or receiving notice of disclaimer under section 7(1)(*b*);

(*b*) on giving a direction revoking the power on exercising any of its powers under Part VII of the Mental Health Act 1983;

(c) on being satisfied that the donor is and is likely to remain mentally capable;

(d) on being satisfied that the power has expired or has been revoked by the death or bankruptcy of the donor or the death, mental incapacity or bankruptcy of the attorney or, if the attorney is a body corporate, its winding up or dissolution;

(e) on being satisfied that the power was not a valid and subsisting enduring power when registration was effected;

(f) on being satisfied that fraud or undue pressure was used to induce the donor or create the power; or

(g) on being satisfied that, having regard to all the circumstances and in particular the attorney's relationship to or connection with the donor, the attorney is unsuitable to be the donor's attorney.

(5) Where the court cancels the registration of an instrument on being satisfied of the matters specified in paragraph (f) or (g) of subsection (4) above it shall by order revoke the power created by the instrument.

(6) On the cancellation of the registration of an instrument under subsection (4) above except paragraph (c) the instrument shall be delivered up to be cancelled, unless the court otherwise directs.

Protection of attorney and third parties

Protection of attorney and third persons where power invalid or revoked

9.—(1) Subsections (2) and (3) below apply where an instrument which did not create a valid power of attorney has been registered under section 6 (whether or not the registration has been cancelled at the time of the act or transaction in question).

(2) Any attorney who acts in pursuance of the power shall not incur any liability (either to the donor or to any other person) by reason of the nonexistence of the power unless at the time of acting he knows—

(a) that the instrument did not create a valid enduring power; or

(b) that an event has occurred which, if the instrument had created a valid enduring power, would have had the effect of revoking the power; or

(c) that, if the instrument had created a valid enduring power, the power would have expired before that time.

(3) Any transaction between the attorney and another person shall, in favour of that person, be as valid as if the power had then been in existence, unless at the time of the transaction that person has knowledge of any of the matters mentioned in subsection (2) above.

(4) Where the interest of a purchaser depends on whether a transaction between the attorney and another person was valid by virtue of subsection (3) above, it shall be conclusively presumed in favour of the purchaser that the transaction was valid if—

    (*a*) the transaction between that person and the attorney was completed within twelve months of the date on which the instrument was registered; or

    (*b*) that person makes a statutory declaration, before or within three months after the completion of the purchase, that he had no reason at the time of the transaction to doubt that the attorney had authority to dispose of the property which was the subject of the transaction.

(5) For the purposes of section 5 of the Powers of Attorney Act 1971 (protection of attorney and third persons where action is taken under the power of attorney in ignorance of its having been revoked) in its application to an enduring power the revocation of which by the donor is by virtue of section (7)(1)(*a*) above invalid unless and until confirmed by the court under section 8(3) above, knowledge of the confirmation of the revocation is, but knowledge of the unconfirmed revocation is not knowledge of the revocation of the power.

(6) Schedule 2 shall have effect to confer protection in cases where the instrument failed to create a valid enduring power and the power has been revoked by the donor's mental incapacity.

(7) In this section 'purchaser' and 'purchase' have the meanings specified in section 205(1) of the Law of Property Act 1925.

Supplementary

Application of Mental Health Act provisions relating to the court

10.—(1) The provisions of Part VII of the Mental Health Act 1983 (relating to the Court of Protection) specified below shall apply to persons within and proceedings under this Act in accordance with the following paragraphs of this subsection and subsection (2) below, that is to say—

    (*a*) section 103 (functions of visitors) shall apply to persons within this Act as it applies to the persons mentioned in that section;

    (*b*) section 104 (powers of judge) shall apply to proceedings under this Act with respect to persons within this Act as it applies to the proceedings mentioned in subsection (1) of that section;

    (*c*) section 105(1) (appeals to nominated judge) shall apply to any decision of the Master of the Court of Protection or any nominated officer in proceedings under this Act as it applies to any decision to which that subsection applies and an appeal shall lie to the Court of Appeal from any decision of a nominated judge whether given in the exercise of his original jurisdiction or on the hearing of an appeal under section 105(1) as extended by this paragraph;

    (*d*) section 106 except subsection (4) (rules of procedure) shall apply to proceedings under this Act and persons within this Act as it applies to the proceedings and persons mentioned in that section.

(2) Any functions conferred or imposed by the provisions of the said Part VII applied by subsection (1) above shall be exercisable also for the purposes

of this Act and the persons who are 'within this Act' are the donors of and attorneys under enduring powers of attorney whether or not they would be patients for the purposes of the said Part VII.

(3) In this section 'nominated judge' and 'nominated officer' have the same meanings as in Part VII of the Mental Health Act 1983.

Application to joint and joint and several attorneys

11.—(1) An instrument which appoints more than one person to be an attorney cannot create an enduring power unless the attorneys are appointed to act jointly or jointly and severally.

(2) This Act, in its application to joint attorneys, applies to them collectively as it applies to a single attorney but subject to the modifications specified in Part I of Schedule 3.

(3) This Act, in its application to joint and several attorneys, applies with the modifications specified in subsections (4) to (7) below and in Part II of Schedule 3.

(4) A failure, as respects any one attorney, to comply with the requirements for the creation of enduring powers, shall prevent the instrument from creating such a power in his case without however affecting its efficacy for that purpose as respects the other or others or its efficacy in his case for the purpose of creating a power of attorney which is not an enduring power.

(5) Where one or more but not both or all the attorneys makes or joins in making an application for registration of the instrument then—

    (*a*) an attorney who is not an applicant as well as one who is may act pending the initial determination of the application as provided in section 1(2) (or under section 5);

    (*b*) notice of the application shall also be given under Schedule 1 to the other attorney or attorneys; and

    (*c*) objection may validly be taken to the registration on a ground relating to an attorney or to the power of an attorney who is not an applicant as well as to one or the power of one who is an applicant.

(6) The court shall not refuse under section 6(6) to register an instrument because a ground of objection to an attorney or power is established if an enduring power subsists as respects some attorney who is not affected thereby but shall give effect to it by the prescribed qualification of the registration.

(7) The court shall not cancel the registration of an instrument under section (8)(4) for any of the causes vitiating registration specified in that subsection if an enduring power subsists as respects some attorney who is not affected thereby but shall give effect to it by the prescribed qualification of the registration.

(8) In this section—

    'prescribed' means prescribed by rules of the court; and

    'the requirements for the creation of enduring powers' means the provisions of section 2 other than subsections (10) to (12) and of regulations under subsection (2) of that section.

Power of Lord Chancellor to modify pre-registration requirements in certain cases

12.—(1) The Lord Chancellor may by order exempt attorneys of such descriptions as he thinks fit from the requirements of this Act to give notice to relatives prior to registration.

(2) Subject to subsection (3) below, where an order is made under this section with respect to attorneys of a specified description then, during the currency of the order, this Act shall have effect in relation to any attorney of that description with the omission of so much of section 4(3) and Schedule 1 as requires notice of an application for registration to be given to relatives.

(3) Notwithstanding that an attorney under a joint or joint and several power is of a description specified in a current order under this section, subsection (2) above shall not apply in relation to him if any of the other attorneys under the power is not of a description specified in that or another current order under this section.

(4) The power to make an order under this section shall be exercisable by statutory instrument which shall be subject to annulment in pursuance of a resolution of either House of Parliament.

Interpretation

13.—(1) In this Act—
'the court', in relation to any functions under this Act, means the authority having jurisdiction under Part VII of the Mental Health Act 1983;
'enduring power' is to be construed in accordance with section 2;
'mentally incapable' or 'mental incapacity', except where it refers to revocation at common law, means, in relation to any person, that he is incapable by reason of mental disorder or managing and administering his property and affairs and 'mentally capable' and 'mental capacity' shall be construed accordingly;
'mental disorder' has the same meaning as it has in the Mental Health Act 1983;
'notice' means notice in writing;
'rules of the court' means rules under Part VII of the Mental Health Act 1983 as applied by section 10;
'statutory maximum' has the meaning given by section 74(1) of the Criminal Justice Act 1982;
'trust corporation' means the Public Trustee or a corporation either appointed by the High Court or a county court (according to their respective jurisdictions) in any particular case to be a trustee or entitled by rules under section 4(3) of the Public Trustee Act 1906 to act as custodian trustee.
(2) Any question arising under or for the purposes of this Act as to what the donor of the power might at any time be expected to do shall be determined by assuming that he had full mental capacity at the time but otherwise by reference to the circumstances existing at that time.

Short title, commencement and extent

14.—(1) This Act may be cited as the Enduring Powers of Attorney Act 1985.

(2) This Act shall come into force on such day as the Lord Chancellor appoints by order made by statutory instrument.

(3) This Act extends to England and Wales only except that section 7(3) and section 10(1)(*b*) so far as it applies section 104(4) of the Mental Health Act 1983 extend also to Scotland and Northern Ireland.

SCHEDULES

SCHEDULE 1

Section 4(3)

NOTIFICATION PRIOR TO REGISTRATION

PART I

DUTY TO GIVE NOTICE TO RELATIVES AND DONOR

Duty to give notice to relatives

1. Subject to paragraph 3 below, before making an application for registration the attorney shall give notice of his intention to do so to all those persons (if any) who are entitled to receive notice by virtue of paragraph 2 below.

2.—(1) Subject to the limitations contained in sub-paragraphs (2) to (4) below, persons of the following classes (referred to in this Act as 'relatives') are entitled to receive notice under paragraph 1 above—

- (*a*) the donor's husband or wife;
- (*b*) the donor's children;
- (*c*) the donor's parents;
- (*d*) the donor's brothers and sisters, whether of the whole or half blood;
- (*e*) the widow or widower of a child of the donor;
- (*f*) the donor's grandchildren;
- (*g*) the children of the donor's brothers and sisters of the whole blood;
- (*h*) the children of the donor's brothers and sisters of the half blood;
- (*i*) the donor's uncle and aunts of the whole blood; and
- (*j*) the children of the donor's uncles and aunts of the whole blood.

(2) A person is not entitled to receive notice under paragraph 1 above if—

- (*a*) his name and address is not known to the attorney and cannot be reasonably ascertained by him; or
- (*b*) the attorney has reason to believe that he has not attained eighteen years or is mentally incapable.

(3) Except where sub-paragraph (4) below applies, no more than three persons are entitled to receive notice under paragraph 1 above and, in determining the persons who are so entitled, persons falling within class (a) of sub-paragraph (1) above are to be preferred to persons falling within class (b) of that sub-paragraph, persons falling within class (b) are to be preferred to persons falling within class (c) of that sub-paragraph; and so on.

(4) Notwithstanding the limit of three specified in sub-paragraph (3) above, where—

(a) there is more than one person falling within any of classes (a) to (j) of sub-paragraph (1) above, and
(b) at least one of those persons would be entitled to receive notice under paragraph 1 above,

then, subject to sub-paragraph (2) above, all the persons falling within that class are entitled to receive notice under paragraph 1 above.

3.—(1) An attorney shall not be required to give notice under paragraph 1 above to himself or to any other attorney under the power who is joining in making the application, notwithstanding that he or, as the case may be, the other attorney is entitled to receive notice by virtue of paragraph 2 above.

(2) In the case of any person who is entitled to receive notice under paragraph 1 above, the attorney, before applying for registration, may make an application to the court to be dispensed from the requirement to give him notice; and the court shall grant the application if it is satisfied—

(a) that it would be undesirable or impracticable for the attorney to give him notice: or
(b) that no useful purpose is likely to be served by giving him notice.

Duty to give notice to donor

4.—(1) Subject to sub-paragraph (2) below, before making an application for registration the attorney shall give notice of his intention to do so to the donor.

(2) Paragraph 3(2) above shall apply in relation to the donor as it applies in relation to a person who is entitled to receive notice under paragraph 1 above.

PART II

CONTENTS OF NOTICES

5. A notice to relatives under this Schedule—

(a) shall be in the prescribed form:
(b) shall state that the attorney proposes to make an application to the Court of Protection for the registration of the instrument creating the enduring power in question;
(c) shall inform the person to whom it is given that he may object to the

proposed registration by notice in writing to the Court of Protection before the expiry of the period of four weeks beginning with the day on which the notice under this Schedule was given him;

(d) shall specify, as the grounds on which an objection to registration may be made, the grounds set out in section 6(5).

6. A notice to the donor under this Schedule—

(a) shall be in the prescribed form;

(b) shall contain the statement mentioned in paragraph 5(b) above; and

(c) shall inform the donor that, whilst the instrument remains registered, any revocation of the power by him will be ineffective unless and until the revocation is confirmed by the Court of Protection.

PART III

DUTY TO GIVE NOTICE TO OTHER ATTORNEYS

7.—(1) Subject to sub-paragraph (2) below, before making an application for registration an attorney under a joint and several power shall give notice of his intention to do so to any other attorney under the power who is not joining in making the application; and paragraphs 3(2) and 5 above shall apply in relation to attorneys entitled to receive notice by virtue of this paragraph as they apply in relation to persons entitled to receive notice of virtue of paragraph 2 above.

(2) An attorney is not entitled to receive notice by virtue of this paragraph if—

(a) his address is not known to the applying attorney and cannot reasonably be ascertained by him; or

(b) the applying attorney has reason to believe that he has not attained eighteen years or is mentally incapable.

PART IV

SUPPLEMENTARY

8.—(1) For the purposes of this Schedule an illegitimate child shall be treated as if he were the legitimate child of his mother and father.

(2) Notwithstanding anything in section 7 of the Interpretation Act 1978 (construction of references to service by post), for the purposes of this Schedule a notice given by post shall be regarded as given on the date on which it was posted.

SCHEDULE 2

Section 9(6)

FURTHER PROTECTION OF ATTORNEY AND THIRD PERSONS

1. Where—

(*a*) an instrument framed in a form prescribed under section 2(2) creates a power which is not a valid enduring power; and

(*b*) the power is revoked by the mental incapacity of the donor, paragraph 2 and 3 below shall apply, whether or not the instrument has been registered.

2. An attorney who acts in pursuance of the power shall not, by reason of the revocation, incur any liability (either to the donor or to any other person) unless at the time of acting he knows—

(*a*) that the instrument did not create a valid enduring power; and

(*b*) that the donor has become mentally incapable.

3. Any transaction between the attorney and another person shall, in favour of that person, be as valid as if the power had then been in existence, unless at the time of the transaction that person knows—

(*a*) that the instrument did not create a valid enduring power; and

(*b*) that the donor has become mentally incapable.

4. Section 9(4) shall apply for the purpose of determining whether a transaction was valid by virtue of paragraph 3 above as it applies for the purpose of determining whether a transaction was valid by virtue of section 9(3).

SCHEDULE 3

Section 11(2),(3)

JOINT AND JOINT AND SEVERAL ATTORNEYS

PART I

JOINT ATTORNEYS

1. In section 2(7), the reference to the time when the attorney executes the instrument shall be read as a reference to the time when the second or last attorney executes the instrument.

2. In section 2(9) and (10), the reference to the attorney shall be read as a reference to any attorney under the power.

3. In section 5, references to the attorney shall be read as including references to any attorney under the power.

4. Section 6 shall have effect as if the ground of objection to the registration of the instrument specified in subsection (5)(*e*) applied to any attorney under the power.

5. In section 8(2), references of the attorney shall be read as including references to any attorney under the power.

6. In section 8(4), references of the attorney shall be read as including references to any attorney under the power.

PART II

JOINT AND SEVERAL ATTORNEYS

7. In section 2(10), the reference to the bankruptcy of the attorney shall be construed as a reference to the bankruptcy of the last remaining attorney under the power; and the bankruptcy of any other attorney under the power shall cause that person to cease to be attorney, whatever the circumstances of the bankruptcy.

8. The restriction upon disclaimer imposed by section 4(6) applies only to those attorneys who have reason to believe that the donor is or is becoming mentally incapable.

Relevant Statutory Instruments

SI 1986 No 126

The Enduring Powers of Attorney (Prescribed Form) Regulations 1986

The Lord Chancellor, in exercise of the powers conferred on him by section 2(2) of the Enduring Powers of Attorney Act 1985 hereby makes the following Regulations:—

Citation and Operation

1. These Regulations may be cited as the Enduring Powers of Attorney (Prescribed Form) Regulations 1986 and shall come into operation on 10th March 1986.

Interpretation

2. In these Regulations unless the context otherwise requires expressions used have the same meaning as in the Act (as herein defined):—
   'the Act' means the Enduring Powers of Attorney Act 1985;
   'attorney' means an attorney appointed under an enduring power of attorney;
   'donor' means a person who has created an enduring power of attorney;
   'enduring power of attorney' means a power of attorney which complies with these Regulations.

Prescribed Form

3.—(1) Subject to regulations 3(2) and 5 of these Regulations, and enduring power of attorney in the form set out in the Schedule to these Regulations, together with such additions, variations or restrictions as the donor may decide, shall operate to confer on the attorney authority to do on behalf of the donor anything which the attorney can lawfully do by virtue of the Act or the contents of the enduring powers of attorney itself.

(2) An enduring power of attorney which seeks to exclude any provision contained in these Regulations, and in particular in the Schedule to these Regulations, is not a valid enduring power of attorney.

Execution

4. An enduring power of attorney in the form set out in the Schedule to these Regulations shall be executed by both the donor and the attorney, although not necessarily at the same time, in the presence of a witness but not necessarily the same witness, who will state his full name, address and occupation. The donor and an attorney may not witness the signature of each other. Where more than one attorney is appointed to act jointly and severally, then at least one of the attorneys so appointed must execute the instrument for it to take effect, but only those attorneys who have executed the instrument shall be able to act under the enduring power of attorney if the donor becomes mentally incapable.

Explanatory Information

5. The prescribed Explanatory Information, set out in the Schedule, shall be endorsed on the enduring power of attorney when the donor executes the instrument.

16th January 1986   *Hailsham of St Marylebone, C*

SCHEDULE

ENDURING POWER OF ATTORNEY
(PRESCRIBED FORM)

THIS ENDURING POWER OF ATTORNEY is made this   day
of   19   by   of
Date of birth
I appoint   of
(and   of
                              jointly or jointly and severally) to be my
attorney(s) for the Enduring Powers of Attorney Act 1985
with general authority to act on my behalf   *or*   with
authority to do the following on my behalf:

in relation to   **(a)**

all my property and affairs   *or*

the following property and affairs: **(b)(c)**

(subject to the following restrictions and conditions):

I intend that this power shall continue even if I become mentally incapable.

I have read *or* had read to me the explanatory information which is endorsed on and explains this document.

IN WITNESS whereof I have hereunto set my hand and seal this   day of   19   in the presence of:—

(d) I/WE, the attorney(s) named in this power understand that under the Enduring Powers of Attorney Act 1985 we have a duty to make application to the Court for the registration of the instrument and have a limited power
(e)(f)(g) (subject to any restrictions or conditions specified in this instrument) to make gifts of property or otherwise to benefit myself/ourselves and other persons and exercise the donor's trust functions. I am/we are not minors.

(h) IN WITNESS whereof the attorney [name] has hereunto set his/her hand and seal this   day of   19   in the presence of:—

IN WITNESS whereof the attorney [name] has hereunto set his/her hand and seal this   day of   19   in the presence of:—

EXPLANATORY INFORMATION

(a) If general authority is given, section 3 of the Enduring Powers of Attorney Act 1985 (the Act) will have the effect, subject to any restrictions or conditions specified in the instrument, of enabling the attorney to do anything the donor can do by an attorney including, for example, selling any house or other property belonging to the donor. He will be able to make gifts and use the donor's property to benefit himself or others, but only to the extent described in notes (e) and (f) below. He may also exercise the donor's trust powers.

(b) If the alternative of giving only limited authority is adopted, the attorney will be able to do only the things specified. However, he will be able to make gifts and use the donor's property to benefit himself or others, but only to the extent described in notes (e) and (f) below or exercise the donor's trust powers, unless the enduring power of attorney restricts this authority.

(c) These further provisions can include, for example, a provision for paying the attorney for his service as attorney.

(d) The duty to apply for the registration of the instrument arises under section 4 of the Act as soon as the attorney has reason to believe the donor is becoming or has become mentally incapable of managing his affairs and is a duty to apply (or join with the other joint attorneys in applying) for the registration of the instrument with the Court of Protection. The Act contains requirements for the notification of the donor and certain of his relatives by the attorney before the instrument can be registered. Details of these requirements are contained in Part 1 of Schedule 1 of the Act.

(e) The donor's property can be given away under an enduring power of attorney within the limits set out in section 3(5) of the Act but it includes power (within those limits) for the attorney to benefit himself by gifts and to exercise the donor's trust powers. The donor can attach conditions to these powers or restrict them further than those limits by inserting the conditions or restrictions in the instrument at the place indicated for any restrictions or conditions. This can include a restriction that the enduring power of attorney is not to come into operation until the attorney has reason to believe that the donor is becoming mentally incapable.

(f) The donor's property can be used to benefit other persons, including the attorney, within the limits set out in section 3(4) of the Act. See also note (e) above as to further restrictions or conditions.

(g) After an instrument has been registered the attorney should notify the Court of Protection of the death or recovery of the donor.

(h) It is inadvisable for a married person to witness the signature to the power of attorney of his or her spouse.

[*The statutory references above have been corrected from the version originally printed*]

SI 1986 No 127

The Court of Protection (Enduring Powers of Attorney) Rules 1986

The Lord Chancellor, in exercise of the powers conferred on him by section 10(1)(*d*) of the Enduring Powers of Attorney Act 1985 and sections 106, 107 and 108 of the Mental Health Act 1983 and with the consent of the Treasury so far as is required by section 106(5) of the said Act of 1983, hereby makes the following Rules:—

PART I

PRELIMINARY

Citation and commencement

1. These Rules may be cited as the Court of Protection (Enduring Powers of Attorney) Rules 1986 and shall come into operation on 10th March 1986.

Application

2. The Court of Protection Rules 1984 and these Rules shall apply equally in proceedings under the Enduring Powers of Attorney Act 1985 save that in cases of inconsistency or ambiguity, the latter shall prevail.

Interpretation

3.—(1) In these Rules, unless the context otherwise requires—expressions used in the Supreme Court Act 1981 have the same meaning as in that Act;
'the 1983 Act' means the Mental Health Act 1983;
'the 1985 Act' means the Enduring Powers of Attorney Act 1985;
'the 1984 Rules' means the Court of Protection Rules 1984;
'applicant' includes an objector;
'application' includes an objector;
'attorney' means an attorney appointed under an enduring power of attorney;
'the court' means the Court of Protection;
'donor' means a person who has created an enduring power of attorney;
'enduring power of attorney' means any power of attorney which complies with the provisions of section 2 of the 1985 Act;
'entered' means entered in the register of enduring powers of attorney kept by the Court of Protection;
'filed' means filed in the court office;
'judge' means the Lord Chancellor or a judge nominated under section 93(1) of the 1983 Act;
'Master' means the Master of the Court of Protection;
'nominated officer' means an officer of the Court of Protection nominated under section 93(4) of the 1983 Act;
'order' includes a certificate, direction or authority under seal;
'receiver' means a receiver appointed under section 99(1) of the 1983 Act;
'relative' means one of the persons referred to as relatives and entitled to receive notice under the provisions of paragraph 1 and 2 of Schedule 1 to the 1985 Act;
'seal' means an official seal of the Court of Protection and 'sealed' shall be construed accordingly; and
'Visitor' means one of the Lord Chancellor's Visitors appointed under section 102 of the 1983 Act.

(2) Where any discretion, power or other function is (in whatever words) expressed by these Rules to be exercisable by 'the court' then subject to the provisions of the 1985 Act, that discretion, power or other function may be exercised—

(a) by a judge;
(b) by the Master; or
(c) to the extent to which he is authorised to exercise it by and under section 94 of the 1983 Act, by a nominated officer.

(3) In these Rules a form referred to by letter means the form so designated in Schedule 1 to these Rules or a form to the like effect with such variations as the circumstances may require and the court may approve.

Computation of time

4.—(1) Any period of time fixed by the 1985 Act or by these Rules or by a judgment, order or direction for doing any act shall be reckoned in accordance with the provisions of this rule.

(2) Where the act is required to be done not less than a specified period before a specified date, the period starts immediately after the date on which the act is done and ends immediately before the specified date.

(3) Where the act is required to be done within a specified period after or from a specified date, the period starts immediately after that date.

(4) Where, apart from this paragraph, the period in question being a period of 3 days or less would include a day on which the court office is closed, that day shall be excluded.

(5) Where the time so fixed for doing an act in the court office expires on a day on which the office is closed, and for that reason the act cannot be done on that day, the act shall be in time if it is done on the next day on which the office is open.

Part II

Applications

Notice of intention to register

5.—(1) Notice of the attorney's intention to apply to register an enduring power of attorney shall be given in Form EP1 to the donor and to those relatives entitled to receive such notice and to any co-attorney.

(2) An application to dispense with such notice shall be made in Form EP3 before any application for registration is made.

Time limits

6.—An application to register an enduring power of attorney shall be made in Form EP2 and shall be lodged with the court not later than three days after the date on which:—
- (a) notice has been given to the donor and every relative (if any) entitled to receive notice and every co-attorney; or
- (b) leave has been given to dispense with notice whichever may be the later.

Form of application

7.—(1) Subject to the provisions of Rules 5 and 6 of these Rules and to the following provisions of this Rule, an application to the court may be by letter unless the court directs that the application should be formal, in which case it shall be made in Form EP3.

(2) An application relating to the committal of a person for contempt of court shall be made to a judge by motion.

Objections to registration

8.—(1) Any objection to registration shall be made in writing and shall set out:—

(*a*) the name and address of the objector;

(*b*) the name and address of the donor, if the objector is not the donor;

(*c*) any relationship of the objector to the donor;

(*d*) the name and address of the attorney; and

(*e*) the grounds for objecting to registration of the enduring power.

(2) Any objection to registration received by the court on or after the date of registration shall be treated by the court as an application to cancel the registration.

Exercise of the court's powers and functions under the provisions of the 1985 Act

9.—(1) This Rule shall apply to applications to the court for relief or for determination of any question under sections 1(1)(*b*), 4(4), 5, 6(3), 6(4), 8(2), 8(3), 8(4) or 11(5)(*c*) of and to any application made under paragraph 3(2), 4(2) or 7(1) of Schedule 1 to the 1985 Act which is not made simultaneously with an application for registration of an enduring power.

(2) Any application made by letter under Rule 7(1) of these Rules other than an objection to registration or disclaimer of attorneyship, shall include the name and address of the applicant, the name of the donor if the applicant is not the donor, the form of relief or determination required and the grounds for the application.

(3) On receipt of an application, the court may decide either that no hearing shall be held or may fix an appointment for directions or for the application to be heard.

(4) The court may at any time, on application or of its own motion, given such directions as it thinks proper with regard to any matter arising in the course of an application.

(5) Notification of an appointment for directions or a hearing shall be given by the applicant to the attorney (if he is not the applicant), to any objector and to any other person directly by the court to be notified.

(6) The applicant, the attorney (if he is not the applicant) and any person given notice of the appointment or hearing may attend or be represented.

(7) If it appears to the court that any order for relief should be made or any question determined, the court may make such order or give such direction as it thinks fit, of its own motion.

(8) Where an enduring power of attorney is sought to be disclaimed pursuant to section 4(6) or 7(1)(*b*) of the 1985 Act, notice of disclaimer by the attorney shall be given in Form EP3 and the disclaimer shall take effect on the day on which the notice of disclaimer is received by the court.

Consolidation of proceedings

10. The court may consolidate any applications for registration or relief or any objections to registration if it considers that the proceedings relating to them can more conveniently be dealt with together.

Registration

11.—(1) Where there is no objection to registration or any objection has been withdrawn or dismissed, the enduring power of attorney shall be registered and sealed.

(2) The court shall retain a copy of the registered enduring power of attorney and shall return the original instrument to the applicant attorney.

(3) Any alterations which are on the face of the instrument when an application for registration is made shall be sealed.

(4) Any qualification to registration imposed by reason of section 11(6) or 11(7) of the 1985 Act shall be noted on the register, and on the instrument, and sealed.

(5) The date of registration shall be the date stamped by the court on the instrument when it is registered.

Searches of the register and copies of registered enduring powers of attorney

12.—(1) Any person shall on payment of the appropriate fee be entitled to request the court in Form EP4 to search the register and to say whether an enduring power of attorney has been registered.

(2) The court may supply any person with an office copy of a registered enduring power of attorney if the court is satisfied that he has good reason for requesting a copy and that it is not reasonably practicable to obtain a copy from the attorney.

(3) For the purposes of this rule, an office copy is a photocopy or a facsimile of an enduring power of attorney, marked as an office copy, sealed and serially numbered.

(4) An office copy of an enduring power of attorney need not contain the Explanatory Information endorsed on the original power.

PART III

HEARINGS

Notice of hearing

13. Except where these Rules otherwise provide or the court otherwise directs, the following periods of notice of a hearing shall be given by the applicant:—

(1) Ten clear day's notice shall be given:—
- (i) in the case of an application to dispense with notice to the donor;
- (ii) in the case of an application to dispose of the donor's property prior to registration; and
- (iii) in the case of an objection to registration of an enduring power,—

unless the court otherwise directs, to the attorney, the donor, every relative as defined in these Rules, to any co-attorney and to such other persons who appear to the court to be interested, as the court may specify.

(2) Seven clear days' notice shall be given in the case of any other application and to any other person interested in the proceedings.

(3) The court may extend or abridge the time limited by these Rules or any order or directions of the court for doing any act or taking any steps, upon such terms as the court thinks fit and notwithstanding in the case of an extension that the time so limited has expired.

(4) For the purposes of this rule notice of hearing is given if the applicant sends a copy of the application to the person concerned.

Mode of service

14.—(1) Any document required by these Rules to be given to the donor shall be given to him personally.

(2) Except where these Rules otherwise provide, any document required by these Rules to be given to any person other than the donor shall be served by sending it to him by first class post.

Service on a solicitor

15. Where a solicitor for the person to be given any document endorses on that document or on a copy of it a statement that he accepts the document on behalf of that person, the document shall be deemed to have been duly sent to that person and to have been received on the date on which the endorsement was made.

Substituted service

16. Where it appears to the court that it is impracticable for any document to be sent in accordance with Rule 14, the court may give such directions for the purpose of bringing the document to the notice of the person to whom it is addressed as it thinks fit.

Use of evidence in subsequent proceedings

17. Except where the court otherwise directs, evidence which has been used in any proceedings relating to a donor may be used at any subsequent stage of those proceedings or in any other proceedings before the court.

Copies of documents in court

18.—(1) Any person who has filed an affidavit or other document shall, unless the court otherwise directs, be entitled on request to be supplied by the court with a copy of it.

(2) An attorney or his solicitor may have a search made for and may inspect and request a copy of any document filed in proceedings relating to the enduring power of attorney under which the attorney has been appointed.

(3) Subject to the foregoing paragraphs, no documents filed in the court office shall be open to inspection without the leave of the court and no copy of

any such document or an extract thereof shall be taken by or issued to any person without such leave.

Summoning of witnesses

19. In any proceedings under these Rules a witness summons shall be issued in Form EP6.

Leave to bring an application

20. Any person other than a person who has been served with a notice of intention to register an enduring power of attorney shall apply to the court for leave to make application for relief specified in the 1985 Act.

Notification of decision

21. All persons who receive notice under Rule 9(5) of these Rules shall be notified by the applicant of the court's decision and shall also be sent by the applicant a copy of any order made or directions given.

PART IV

REVIEWS AND APPEALS

Review of a decision by a nominated officer

22.—(1) Any person who is aggrieved by a decision of a nominated officer may apply to the court within eight days of the date on which the decision was given to have the decision reviewed by the Master.

(2) No application for review shall lie from any decision in relation to the exercise of the court's power under Rule 83 of the 1984 Rules.

(3) On reviewing the decision, the Master may confirm or revoke the decision or may make or give any other order or decision.

Appeal from the Master

23.—(1) Any person aggrieved by any order or decision of the Master may, within fourteen days from the date of entry of the order or, as the case may be, from the date of the decision, appeal therefrom to a judge.

(2) The appellant shall, within the said period of fourteen days—
   (*a*) serve notice of appeal in Form EP7 on every person who is directly affected by the decision, and any other person whom the court may direct; and
   (*b*) lodge a copy of the notice at the court office.

(3) The time and place at which the appeal is to be heard shall be fixed by the court, and an officer of the court shall cause notice of the time and place so fixed to be sent to the appellant who shall forthwith send notice thereof to every person who has been served with notice of appeal.

(4) No further evidence shall be filed in support of or opposition to the appeal without leave of the judge.

(5) No appeal shall lie from any order or decision which was not made or given on a hearing.

Part V

Cancellation of Registration

Cancellation of a registered enduring power of attorney

24.—(1) Where the court is satisfied that one of the circumstances listed in section 8(4) of the 1985 Act applies, it shall cancel the registration of the enduring power of attorney in question and shall send a notice to the attorney requiring him to deliver to the court the original instrument.

(2) Where the instrument creating an enduring power of attorney has been lost or destroyed, the person on whom notice under paragraph 1 of this Rule has been served shall give to the court written details of the date on which the instrument was lost or destroyed and the circumstances in which that occurred.

(3) Where the court has cancelled the registration of an instrument because it is satisfied that:—

(a) fraud or undue pressure was used to induce the donor to create the power, or

(b) having regard to all the circumstances and in particular the attorney's relationship to or connection with the donor, the attorney is unsuitable to be the donor's attorney,

the court shall revoke the power created by the instrument.

(4) Where registration has been cancelled for any reason other than one of those set out in paragraph 3(a) or (b) of this Rule or section 8(4)(c) of the 1985 Act, the court shall mark the power of attorney as cancelled.

(5) Any notices issued by the court under this Rule may contain a warning that failure to comply with the notice may lead to punishment for contempt of court.

Part VI

Fees

Schedule of Fees

25.—(1) Fees shall be payable in accordance with the provisions of Schedule 2.

(2) The fee set out in column 2 of Schedule 2 shall be taken in respect of the event referred to in column 1.

(3) Unless the court otherwise directs, all fees shall be taken in cash.

(4) The person by whom any fee is payable shall, unless the fee is for a

search of the register or unless the court otherwise directs, make the payment out of the assets of the donor.

Registration fee

26. A fee shall be payable on any application for registration of an enduring power of attorney.

Dated 16th January 1982 *Hailsham of St Marylebone, C*

We concur.

A G Hamilton,
T Garel-Jones,
Two of the Lord Commissioners
Dated 27th January 1986 of Her Majesty's Treasury

[*The Court Rules as printed here include typographical corrections to the version originally printed*]

APPENDIX 2

SCHEDULE 1

FORM EP1

NOTICE OF INTENTION TO APPLY FOR REGISTRATION

Court of Protection

Enduring Powers of Attorney Act 1985

Rule 5

Notice of intention to apply for registration

TAKE NOTICE THAT

I (we) _____

_____

of _____

_____

the attorney(s) of _____

_____

of _____

_____

intend to apply to the Court of Protection for
registration of the enduring power of attorney
appointing me(us) attorney(s) and made by the
donor on the _____ 19_____

1 You have 4 weeks from the day on which this notice is given to
   you to object in writing to the proposed registration of the
   power of attorney. Objections should be sent to the Court of
   Protection and should contain the following details:

   • your name and address;

   • any relationship to the donor;

   • if you are not the donor, the name and address of the
     donor;

   • the name and address of the attorney;

   • the grounds for objecting to the registration of the
     enduring power.

Note. The instrument means the enduring power of attorney made by the donor which it is sought to register.

2   The grounds on which you may object are:

- that the power purported to have been created by the instrument is not valid as an enduring power of attorney;

- that the power created by the instrument no longer subsists;

- that the application is premature because the donor is not yet becoming mentally incapable;

- that fraud or undue pressure was used to induce the donor to make the power;

- that the attorney is unsuitable to be the donor's attorney (having regard to all the circumstances and in particular the attorney's relationship to or connection with the donor).

Note. Cross this part out if the notice is not addressed to the donor

3   You are informed that while the enduring power of attorney remains registered, you will not be able to revoke it until the Court of Protection confirms the revocation.

Note. The notice should be signed by all the attorneys who are applying to register the enduring power of attorney.

Signed _____

Signed _____

Dated _____

APPENDIX 2

FORM EP2

APPLICATION FOR REGISTRATION

Court of Protection   No. _____

Enduring Powers of Attorney Act 1985

Rule 6

> Application for registration

> **The attorney(s)**
> Name(s)_____
> _____
> age_____ occupation _____
> age_____ occupation _____
> address(es) _____
> _____
> _____

Note Give the full name(s) of the attorney(s)

Note. Give the full name and present address of the donor. If the donor's address on the enduring power of attorney is different give that one too.

> **The donor**
> Name _____
> address _____
> _____
> _____

> I(we) the attorney(s) apply to register the enduring power
> of attorney made by the donor under the above Act on
> the _____ 19_____ _____

> I(we) have reason to believe that the donor is or is
> becoming mentally incapable.

> I(we) have given notice in the prescribed form to the
> following:
>   • the donor personally at _____
>   _____
>   on the _____ 19_____

- **The following relatives of the donor at the addresses below on the dates given:**
  Names   Relationship   address   date

Note Cross out this section if it does not apply.

- The Co-Attorney _____

  at _____

  on _____

The Enduring Power of Attorney accompanies this application

Note. The application should be signed by all the attorneys who are making the application.

I(we) certify that the above information is correct and that to the best of my(our) knowledge and belief I(we) have complied with the provisions of the Enduring Powers of Attorney Act 1985 and of all the Rules and Regulations under it.

Signed _____

Signed _____

Dated _____

Address where notice should be sent _____

_____

APPENDIX 2

FORM EP3

GENERAL FORM OF APPLICATION

Court of Protection   No _____

Enduring Powers of Attorney Act 1985

In the matter of a power given by

_____ a donor

to _____ attorney(s)

Rule 7(1)

> General form of application

I(we) _____

of _____

_____

Note. Give details of the order that you are asking the court to make.

apply for an order that

_____

_____

_____

_____

_____

and for any directions which are necessary as a result of my(our) application.

Note. Give details of the grounds on which you are asking the court to make the order

The grounds on which I(we) make this application are.

_____

_____

_____

_____

_____

Note. The application should be signed by all the applicants or their solicitors.

Signed _____

Dated _____

Address where notice should be sent _____

_____

_____

FORM EP4

APPLICATION FOR SEARCH/OFFICE COPY

Court of Protection   No _____

Enduring Powers of Attorney Act 1985

Rule 12

Application for search/office copy

I(we) _____

of _____

_____

apply to be informed by the Court whether an enduring power of

attorney has been registered (or whether registration of an

enduring power of attorney is pending) in the name of:

Note Give the full name (if known) of the person who is the subject of your enquiry.

_____

alternative name _____

address (if known) _____

_____

alternative address _____

I(we) enclose the prescribed fee of £_____

Note Please fill in if applicable

Please supply me with an office copy of the power.

- My(Our) reasons for requesting a copy from the Court are

_____

_____

_____

_____

- It is not reasonably practicable to obtain a copy from the

attorney because: _____

_____

_____

_____

Signed _____

Dated _____

APPENDIX 2

FORM EP5

CERTIFICATE OF RESULT OF SEARCH

Court of Protection   No _____

Enduring Powers of Attorney Act 1985

Certificate of result of search

In reply to your enquiry

☐ The following enduring power of attorney is registered against the donor's name you give:

Donor's name _____

Attorney's name(s) _____

Power made by donor on _____ registered on _____

☐ There is an application pending for registration of the following enduring power of attorney:

Donor's name _____

Attorney's name(s) _____

Power made by donor on _____

☐ There was an enduring power of attorney registered against the donor's name you give but the registration has been cancelled (and revoked)

Donor's name _____

Attorney's name(s) _____

Power made by donor on _____ registered on _____

Date cancelled (and revoked) _____

☐ There is no enduring power of attorney registered against the donor's name you give.

Signed _____

Dated _____

FORM EP6

Court of Protection   No _____

Enduring Powers of Attorney Act 1985

In the matter of a power given by

_____a donor

Rule 19

> **Witness summons**

To _____

of _____

_____

you are ordered to attend before

_____

at_____

_____

on the _____day of _____19_____

at_____ o'clock, to:

- give evidence in this matter
- bring with you and produce at the hearing the documents
  listed below:

_____

_____

_____

_____

_____

Dated _____

This summons was issued at the request of

_____

Solicitors for the _____

of _____

_____

APPENDIX 2

FORM EP7

NOTICE OF APPEAL

Court of Protection   No _____

Enduring Powers of Attorney Act 1985

In the matter of a power given by

_____a donor

Rule 23

> Notice of appeal

I(we)_____

of _____

_____

wish to appeal to a judge against the order/decision of the Court

> **Note.** If you are appealing against only part of the order/decision write down which part.

made in this matter on the _____19____

_____

_____

_____

_____

> **Note.** Tick the box that applies.

I(We) intend to ask that the order/decision may be

> **Note.** Give details of the new order/decision you are asking to be made.

☐ discharged

☐ varied in the following way

_____

_____

_____

_____

_____

> **Note.** The form should be sent to the Court of Protection.

Signed _____appellant

Dated _____

Solicitors for the appellant(s) _____

of _____

_____

> **To the appellants: you will be sent notice of the time, date and place of this appeal.**

SCHEDULE 2

FEES

Rule 25

Column 1	Column 2
Item	Fee
Registration fee (rule 26)	
1.—On lodging an application for registration of an enduring power of attorney	£30.00
Search fee (rule 12)	
2. On application for a search of the register	£5.00

1986 No 1537

The Land Registration (Powers of Attorney) Rules 1986

The Lord Chancellor, with the advice and assistance of the Rule Committee appointed in pursuance of section 144 of the Land Registration Act 1925, in exercise of the powers conferred on him by that section, hereby makes the following Rules:—

1. These Rules may be cited as the Land Registration (Powers of Attorney) Rules 1986 and shall come into operation on 1st October 1986.

2. The following rule shall be substituted for Rule 82 of the Land Registration Rules 1925:—

'**82.**—(1) If any instrument executed by an attorney is delivered at the Registry, there shall be furnished to the registrar either the instrument creating the power of attorney, or a copy by means of which its contents may be proved under either section 3 of the Powers of Attorney Act 1971 or section 7(3) of the Enduring Powers of Attorney Act 1985 or a document which complies with section 4 of the Evidence and Powers of Attorney Act 1940.

(2) If an Order pursuant to section 8 of the Enduring Powers of Attorney Act 1985 has been made with respect to a power or the donor thereof or the attorney appointed thereunder the order or an office copy or copy certified pursuant to rule 309 shall be furnished to the registrar.

(3) The registrar may retain any instrument creating a power of attorney or any order or any copy or document produced pursuant to this rule.

(4) If any transaction between the donee of a power of attorney and the person dealing with him is not completed within twelve months of the date on which the power came into operation, evidence shall be produced to the registrar to satisfy him that the power had not been revoked at the time of the transaction.

(5) When the power was in a form prescribed under section 2(2) of the Enduring Powers of Attorney Act 1985 the evidence that the power had not been revoked shall, unless the registrar otherwise directs, consist of a statutory declaration by the person dealing with the donee of the power that he did not, at the time of the completion of the transaction:

    (*a*) know of any revocation of the power whether by the donor or by an Order of the Court Protection

(b) know of the occurrence of any event (such as the death of the donor or the bankruptcy of the donor or of any donee or a direction by the Court of Protection on exercising its powers under Part VII of the Mental Health Act 1983 which had the effect of revoking the power

(c) know that the power was not a valid enduring power of attorney and had been revoked by the donor's mental incapacity.

(6) In any case to which paragraph (5) above does not apply the evidence that the power has not been revoked shall, unless the registrar otherwise directs, consist of a statutory declaration by the person dealing with the donee that he did not, at the time of the completion of the transaction:

(a) know of any revocation of the power

(b) know of the occurrence of any event (such as the death, bankruptcy or other incapacity of the donor) which had the effect of revoking the power.

Provided that where the power was expressed in the instrument creating it to be irrevocable and to be given by way of security the statutory declaration shall be to the effect that the declarant did not know that the power was not in fact given by way of security and did not know that the power had been revoked by the donor acting with the consent of the donee.'

3. The Land Registration (Powers of Attorney) Rules 1971 are hereby revoked.

Dated 3rd September 1986 *Hailsham of St Marlyebone, C.*

SI No 1925

Insolvency Rules 1986, Part 8 and Forms 8.1–8.5

PART 8

PROXIES AND COMPANY REPRESENTATION

Definition of 'proxy'

8.1—(1) For the purposes of the Rules, a proxy is an authority given by a person ('the principal') to another person ('the proxy-holder') to attend a meeting and vote as his representative.

(2) Proxies are for use at creditors', company or contributories' meetings under the Act or the Rules.

(3) Only one proxy may be given by a person for any one meeting at which he desires to be represented; and it may only be given to one person, being an individual aged 18 or over. But the principal may specify one or more other such individuals to be proxy-holder in the alternative, in the order in which they are named in the proxy.

(4) Without prejudice to the generality of paragraph (3), a proxy for a particular meeting may be given to whoever is to be the chairman of the meeting; and for a meeting held as part of the proceedings in a winding up by the court, or in a bankruptcy, it may be given to the official receiver.

(5) A proxy requires the holder to give the principal's vote on matters arising for determination at the meeting, or to abstain, either as directed or in accordance with the holder's own discretion; and it may authorise or require the holder to propose, in the principal's name, a resolution to be voted on by the meeting.

Issue and use of forms

8.2—(1) When notice is given of a meeting to be held in insolvency proceedings, and forms of proxy are sent out with the notice, no form so sent out shall have inserted in it the name or description of any person.

(2) No form of proxy shall be used at any meeting except that which is sent out with the notice summoning the meeting, or a substantially similar form.

(3) A form of proxy shall be signed by the principal, or by some person authorised by him (either generally or with reference to a particular meeting).

172

If the form is signed by a person other than the principal, the nature of the person's authority shall be stated.

Use of proxies at meetings

8.3—(1) A proxy given for a particular meeting may be used at any adjournment of that meeting.

(2) Where the official receiver holds proxies for use at any meeting, his deputy, or any other official receiver, may act as proxy-holder in his place. Alternatively, the official receiver may in writing authorise another officer of the Department to act for him at the meeting and use the proxies as if that other officer were himself proxy-holder.

(3) Where the responsible insolvency practitioner holds proxies to be used by him as chairman of a meeting, and some other person acts as chairman, the other person may use the insolvency practitioner's proxies as if he were himself proxy-holder.

Retention of proxies

8.4—(1) Subject as follows, proxies used for voting at any meeting shall be retained by the chairman of the meeting.

(2) The chairman shall deliver the proxies, forthwith after the meeting, to the responsible insolvency practitioner (where that is someone other than himself).

Right of inspection

8.5—(1) The responsible insolvency practitioner shall, so long as proxies lodged with him are in his hands, allow them to be inspected, at all reasonable times on any business day, by—

  (a) the creditors, in the case of proxies used at a meeting of creditors, and

  (b) a company's members or contributories, in the case of proxies used at a meeting of the company or of its contributories.

(2) The reference in paragraph (1) to creditors is—

  (a) in the case of a company in liquidation or of an individual's bankruptcy, those creditors who have proved their debts, and

  (b) in any other case, persons who have submitted in writing a claim to be creditors of the company or individual concerned;

but in neither case does it include a person whose proof or claim has been wholly rejected for purposes of voting, dividend or otherwise.

(3) The right of inspection given by this Rule is also exercisable—

  (a) in the case of an insolvent company, by its directors, and

  (b) in the case of an insolvent individual, by him.

(4) Any person attending a meeting in insolvency proceedings is entitled, immediately before or in the course of the meeting, to inspect the proxies and associated documents to be used in connection with that meeting.

Proxy-holder with financial interest

8.6—(1) A proxy-holder shall not vote in favour of any resolution which would directly or indirectly place him, or any associate of his, in a position to receive any remuneration out of the insolvent estate, unless the proxy specifically directs him to vote in that way.

(2) This Rule applies also to any person acting as chairman of a meeting and using proxies in that capacity; and in its application to him, the proxy-holder is deemed an associate of his.

Company representation

8.7—(1) Where a person is authorised under section 375 of the Companies Act to represent a corporation at a meeting of creditors or of the company or its contributories, he shall produce to the chairman of the meeting a copy of the resolution from which he derives his authority.

(2) The copy resolution must be under the seal of the corporation, or certified by the secretary or a director of the corporation to be a true copy.

Rule 8.1 Insolvency Act 1986

Proxy (Company or Individual Voluntary Arrangements)

(TITLE)

Notes to help completion of the form

Please give full name and address for communication

Name of creditor/member _____

Address _____

_____

Please insert name of person (who must be 18 or over) or the "chairman of the meeting" (see note below). If you wish to provide for alternative proxy-holders in the circumstances that your first choice is unable to attend please state the name(s) of the alternative as well

Name of proxy-holder _____

1 _____

_____

2 _____

_____

3 _____

_____

Please delete words in brackets if the proxy-holder is only to vote as directed ie he has no discretion

I appoint the above person to be my/the creditor's/member's proxy-holder at the meeting of creditors/members to be held on _____ , or at any adjournment of that meeting. The proxy-holder is to propose or vote as instructed below [and in respect of any resulution for which no specific instruction is given, may vote or abstain at his/her discretion].

Voting instructions for resolutions

*Please delete as appropriate

1. For the acceptance/rejection* of the proposed voluntary arrangement [with the following modifications:—]

Any other resolutions which the proxy-holder is to propose or vote in favour of or against should be set out in numbered paragraphs in the space provided below. Paragraph 1. If more room is required please use the other side of this form.

_____

_____

_____

_____

_____

_____

This form must be signed

Signature _____ Date _____

Name in CAPITAL LETTERS _____

Only to completed if the creditor/member has not signed in person

Position with creditor/member or relationship to creditor/member or other authority for signature _____

_____

Remember: there may be resolutions on the other side of this form.

Rule 8.1   Insolvency Act 1986
Proxy Administration

(TITLE)

Notes to help completion
of the form

Please give full name and
address for communication

Name of creditor/member _____

Address _____

_____

_____

Please insert name of
person (who must be 18 or
over) or the "chairman of
the meeting". If you wish
to provide for alternative
proxy-holders in the
circumstances that your
first choice is unable to
attend please state the
name(s) of the alternative
as well

Name of proxy-holder _____

1 _____

_____

_____

_____

2 _____

_____

_____

_____

3 _____

Please delete words in
brackets if the proxy-holder
is only to vote as directed
ie he has no discretion

I appoint the above person to be my/the creditor's/member's
proxy-holder at the meeting of creditors/members to be held
on _____ , or at any adjournment of that
meeting. The proxy-holder is to propose or vote as instructed
below [and in respect of any resulution for which no specific
instruction is given, may vote or abstain at his/her discretion].

Voting instructions for resolutions

*Please delete as
appropriate

1. For the acceptance/rejection* of the administrator's
   proposals* as circulated

_____ _____

_____

_____

2. For the appointment of _____ of _____

_____

_____

representing _____

as a member of the creditors' committee

This form must be signed

Signature _____ Date _____

Name in CAPITAL LETTERS _____

Only to completed if the
creditor has not signed in
person

Position with creditor or relationship to creditor or other
authority for signature

_____

Remember: there may be resolutions on the other
side of this form.

Rule 8.1   Insolvency Act 1986

Proxy (Administrative Receivership)

(TITLE)

Notes to help completion of the form

Please give full name and address for communication

Name of creditor/member _____

Address _____

_____

_____

Please insert name of person (who must be 18 or over) or the "chairman of the meeting". If you wish to provide for alternative proxy-holders in the circumstances that your first choice is unable to attend please state the name(s) of the alternative as well

Name of proxy-holder _____

_____

_____

_____

_____

_____

_____

_____

_____

_____

_____

Please delete words in brackets if the proxy-holder is only to vote as directed ie he has no discretion

I appoint the above person to be my/the creditor's/member's proxy-holder at the meeting of creditors/members to be held on _____ , or at any adjournment of that meeting. The proxy-holder is to propose or vote as instructed below [and in respect of any resulution for which no specific instruction is given, may vote or abstain at his/her discretion].

_____

Voting instructions for resolutions

for the appointment of _____

of _____

representing _____

representing _____

as a member of the creditors' committee

This form must be signed

Signature _____ Date _____

Name in CAPITAL LETTERS _____

Only to completed if the creditor has not signed in person

Position with creditor or relationship to creditor or other authority for signature

_____

Remember: there may be resolutions on the other side of this form.

APPENDIX 2

Insolvency Act 1986

Proxy (Winding up by the Court or Bankruptcy)

(TITLE)

Notes to help completion of the form	
Please give full name and address for communication	Name of creditor/member _____ Address _____ _____ _____
Please insert name of person (who must be 18 or over) or the "Official Receiver". If you wish to provide for alternative proxy-holders in the circumstances that your first choice is unable to attend please state the name(s) of the alternative as well	Name of proxy-holder _____ 1 _____ _____ _____ 2 _____ _____ _____ 3 _____ _____ _____
Please delete words in brackets if the proxy-holder is only to vote as directed ie he has no discretion	I appoint the above person to be my/the creditor's/ contributory's proxy-holder at the meeting of creditors/ contributories to be held on _____ , or at any adjournment of that meeting. The proxy-holder is to propose or vote as instructed below [and in respect of any resulution for which no specific instruction is given, may vote or abstain at his/her discretion].

Please complete paragraph 1 if you wish to nominate or vote for a specific person as trustee/liquidator

Voting instructions for resolutions

1. For the appointment of _____ of _____

_____

as liquidator of the company/trustee of the bankrupt's estate.

Please delete words in brackets if the proxy-holder is only to vote as directed ie he has no discretion

[in the event of a person named in paragraph 1 withdrawing or being eliminated from any vote for the appointment of a liquidator/trustee the proxy-holder may vote or abstain in any further ballot at his/her discretion]

Any other resolutions which the proxy-holder is to propose or vote in favour of or against should be set out in numbered paragraphs in the space provided below paragraph 1. If more room is required please use the other side of this form.

_____

_____

_____

_____

_____

_____

_____

_____

_____

_____

_____

This form must be signed

Signature _____ Date _____

Name in CAPITAL LETTERS _____

Only to completed if the creditor/member has not signed in person

Position with creditor/member or relationship to creditor/ member or other authority for signature _____

_____

_____

Remember: there may be resolutions on the other side of this form.

Rule 8.1   Insolvency Act 1986

Proxy (Members' or Creditors' Voluntary Winding Up)

(TITLE)

Notes to help completion of the form

Please give full name and address for communication

Name of creditor/member _____

Address _____

_____

_____

Please insert name of person (who must be 18 or over) or the "chairman of the meeting" (see note below). If you wish to provide for alternative proxy-holders in the circumstances that your first choice is unable to attend please state the name(s) of the alternative as well

Name of proxy-holder _____

1 _____

_____

_____

2 _____

_____

_____

3 _____

_____

_____

Please delete words in brackets if the proxy-holder is only to vote as directed ie he has no discretion

I appoint the above person to be my/the creditor's/ contributory's proxy-holder at the meeting of creditors/ contributories to be held on _____ , or at any adjournment of that meeting. The proxy-holder is to propose or vote as instructed below [and in respect of any resulution for which no specific instruction is given, may vote or abstain at his/her discretion].

_____

Please complete
paragraph 1 if you
wish to nominate or
vote for a specific person
as trustee/liquidator

Voting instructions for resolutions

1. For the appointment of _____ of _____

_____

Please delete words in
brackets if the proxy-holder
is only to vote as directed
ie he has no discretion

as liquidator of the company

[in the event of a person named in paragraph 1 withdrawing
or being eliminated from any vote for the appointment of a
liquidator/trustee the proxy-holder may vote or abstain in any
further ballot at his/her discretion]

Any other resolutions
which the proxy-holder is
to propose or vote in
favour of or against should
be set out in numbered
paragraphs in the space
provided below paragraph
1. If more room is required
please use the other side of
this form.

_____

_____

_____

_____

_____

_____

_____

_____

_____

This form must be signed

Signature _____ Date _____

Name in CAPITAL LETTERS _____

Only to completed if the
creditor/member has not
signed in person

Position with creditor/member or relationship to creditor/
member or other authority for signature _____

_____

_____

Please note that if you nominate the chairman of the
meeting to be your proxy-holder he will either be a
director of the company or the current liquidator.

Remember: there may be resolutions on the other
side of this form.

1987 No 1612

The Enduring Powers of Attorney (Prescribed Form) Regulations 1987

The Lord Chancellor, in exercise of the power conferred on him by section 2(2) of the Enduring Powers of Attorney Act 1985, hereby makes the following Regulations:

Citation and commencement

1. These Regulations may be cited as the Enduring Powers of Attorney (Prescribed Form) Regulations 1987 and shall come into force on 1st November 1987.

Prescribed Form

2.—(1) Subject to paragraph (2) and (3) of this regulation and to regulation 4, an enduring power of attorney must be in the form set out in the Schedule to these Regulations and must include all the explanatory information headed 'About using this form' in Part A of the Schedule and all the relevant marginal notes to Parts B and C. It may also include such additions or restrictions as the donor may decide.

(2) In completing the form of enduring power of attorney, the donor shall exclude (either by omission or deletion) one and only one of any pair of alternatives. When one of a pair of alternatives is omitted or deleted, the corresponding marginal note may be omitted or deleted.

(3) The form of execution by an attorney of an enduring power of attorney may be adapted to provide for sealing by a trust corporation with its common seal.

(4) Subject to paragraph (1), (2) and (3) of this regulation and to regulation 4, an enduring power of attorney which seeks to exclude any provision contained in these Regulations is not a valid enduring power of attorney.

Execution

3. An enduring power of attorney in the form set out in the Schedule to these Regulations shall be executed by both the donor and the attorney, although not necessarily at the same time, in the presence of a witness, but not necessarily the same witness, who shall give his full name and address. The donor and an attorney shall not witness the signature of each other nor one attorney the signature of another. Where more than one attorney is appointed and they are to act jointly and severally, then at least one of the attorneys so appointed must execute the instrument for it to take effect as an enduring power of attorney, but only those attorneys who have executed the instrument shall be able to act under the enduring power of attorney in the event of the donor's mental incapacity or of the registration of the power, whichever first occurs.

Revocation

4. The Enduring Powers of Attorney (Prescribed Form) Regulations 1986 are hereby revoked, except that a power executed in the form prescribed by those Regulations and executed before 1st July 1988 shall be capable of being a valid enduring power of attorney.

Dated 1st September 1987 *Havers, C.*

SCHEDULE
ENDURING POWER OF ATTORNEY

Part A: About using this form

1 You may choose one attorney or more than one. If you choose more than one, you must decide whether they are to be able to act:
    Jointly (that is, they must all act together and cannot act separately) or
    Jointly and severally (that is, they can all act together but they can also act separately if they wish.
On the form, at the place marked **1**, show what you have decided by crossing out one of the alternatives.
    2 If you give your attorney(s) general power in relation to all your property and affairs, it means that they will be able to deal with your money or property and may be able to sell your house.
    3 If you don't want your attorney(s) to have such wide powers, you can include any restrictions you like. For example, you can include a restriction that your attorney(s) must not act on your behalf until they have reason to believe that you are becoming mentally incapable; or a restriction that your attorney(s) may not sell your house. Any restrictions you choose must be written or typed on the form in the place marked **2**.
    4 Unless you put in a restriction preventing it your attorney(s) will be able to use any of your money or property to benefit themselves or other people by doing what you yourself might be expected to do to provide for their needs. Your attorney(s) will also be able to use your money to make gifts, but only for reasonable amounts in relation to the value of your money and property.

5 Your attorney(s) can recover the out-of-pocket expenses of acting as your attorney(s). If your attorney(s) are professional people, for example solicitors or accountants, they may be able to charge for their professional services as well.

6 If your attorney(s) have reason in the future to believe that you have become or are becoming mentally incapable of managing your affairs, your attorney(s) will have to apply to the Court of Protection for registration of this power.

7 Before applying to the Court of Protection for registration of this power, your attorney(s) must give written notice that that is what they are going to do, to you and your nearest relatives as defined in the Enduring Powers of Attorney Act 1985. You or your relatives will be able to object if you or they disagree with registration.

8 This is a simplified explanation of what the Enduring Powers of Attorney Act 1985 and the Rules and Regulations say. If you need more guidance, you or your advisers will need to look at the Act itself and the Rules and Regulations. The Rules are the Court of Protection (Enduring Powers of Attorney) Rules 1986 (Statutory Instrument 1986 No 127). The Regulations are the Enduring Powers of Attorney (Prescribed Form) Regulations 1987 (Statutory Instrument 1987 No 1612).

9 *Note to Attorney(s)*: After the power has been registered the attorney(s) should notify the Court of Protection if the donor dies or recovers.

You can cancel this power at any time before it has to be registered.

Part B: To be completed by the 'donor' (the person appointing the attorney(s))

Don't sign this form unless you understand what it means
Please read the notes
in the margin

Donor's name and
address

Donor's date of birth   born on

Attorney(s) name(s)   appoint
and address(es)
                        of

See note 1. If you are   [and
appointing only one
attorney you should   of
cross out everything
between the square
brackets

Cross out the one   1 ● jointly
which does not apply   ● jointly and severally]
(see note 1)
                        to be my attorney(s) for the purpose of the
                        Enduring Powers of Attorney Act 1985

Cross out the one which does not apply (see note 2)

- with general authority to act on my behalf
- with authority to do the following on my behalf:

If you don't want the attorney(s) to have general power, you must give details here of what authority you are giving the attorney(s)

Cross out the one which does not apply

in relation to
- all my property and affairs
- the following property and affairs:

Please read the notes in the margin

If there are restrictions or conditions, insert them here; if not, cross out these words (See note 3)

2 ● subject to the following restrictions and conditions:

I intend that this power shall continue even if I become mentally incapable.

I have read or have had read to me the notes in Part A which are part of, and explain, this form.

Your signature

Signed, sealed and delivered by me _____ L.S.

Date

on _____

Someone must witness your signature

Signature of witness

In the presence of _____

Your attorney(s) cannot be your witness. If you are married it is not advisable for your husband or wife to be your witness

Full name of witness _____

Address of witness _____

_____

_____

_____

SUPERSEDED

Part C: To be completed by the attorney(s)

Note: This form may be adapted to provide for sealing by a corporation with its common seal

If there are more than two attorneys attach an additional Part C.

Don't sign this form before the donor has signed Part B	I understand that I have a duty to apply to the Court for the registration of this form under the Enduring Powers of Attorney Act 1985 when the donor is becoming or has become mentally incapable.
	I also understand my limited power to use the donor's property to benefit persons other than the donor.
	I am not a minor
Signature of attorney	Signed, sealed and delivered by me _____ L.S.
Date	on _____
Signature of witness	in the presence of _____
Each attorney must sign the form and each signature must be witnessed. The donor may not be the witness and one attorney may not witness the signature of the other	Full name of the witness _____
	Address of witness _____
	_____
	_____
	_____
	_____
To be completed only if there is a second attorney	I understand that I have a duty to apply to the Court for the registration of this form under the Enduring Powers of Attorney Act 1985 when the donor is becoming or has become mentally incapable.
	I also understand my limited power to use the donor's property to benefit persons other than the donor.
	I am not a minor
Signature of attorney	Signed, sealed and delivered by me _____ L.S.
Date	on _____
Signature of witness	in the presence of _____

Each attorney must
sign the form and
each signature must
be witnessed. The
donor may not be the
witness and one
attorney may not
witness the signature
of the other

Full name of witness _____

Address of witness _____

_____

_____

_____

_____

SUPERSEDED

The Non-Contentious Probate Rules 1987, rr 31, 35

Grants to attorneys

31.—(1) Subject to paragraphs (2) and (3) below, the lawfully constituted attorney of a person entitled to a grant may apply for administration for the use and benefit of the donor, and such grant shall be limited until further representation be granted, or in such other way as the registrar may direct.

(2) Where the donor referred to in paragraph (1) above is an executor, notice of the application shall be given to any other executor unless such notice is dispensed with by the registrar.

(3) Where the donor referred to in paragraph (1) above is mentally incapable and the attorney is acting under an enduring power of attorney, the application shall be made in accordance with rule 35.

Grants in case of mental incapacity

35.—(1) Unless a registrar otherwise directs, no grant shall be made under this rule unless all persons entitled in the same degree as the incapable person referred to in paragraph (2) below have been cleared off.

(2) Where a registrar is satisfied that a person entitled to a grant is by reason of mental incapacity incapable of managing his affairs, adminstration for his use and benefit, limited until further representation be granted or in such other way as the registrar may direct, may be granted in the following order of priority—

(a) to the person authorised by the Court of Protection to apply for a grant;

(b) where there is no persons so authorised, to the lawful attorney of the incapable person acting under a registered enduring power of attorney;

(c) where there is no such attorney entitled to act, or if the attorney shall renounce adminstration for the use and benefit of the incapable person, to the person entitled to the residuary estate of the deceased.

(3) Where a grant is required to be made to not less than two administrators, and there is only one person competent and willing to take a grant under the foregoing provisions of this rule, administration may, unless a registrar otherwise directs, be granted to such·person jointly with any other person nominated by him.

(4) Notwithstanding the foregoing provisions of this rule, adminstration for the use and benefit of the incapable person may be granted to such two or more other persons as the registrar may by order direct.

(5) Notice of an intended application under this rule shall be given to the Court of Protection.

1990 No 1376

The Enduring Powers of Attorney (Prescribed Form) Regulations 1990

The Lord Chancellor, in exercise of the powers conferred on him by section 2(2) of the Enduring Powers of Attorney Act 1985 (**a**), hereby makes the following Regulations:

Citation and commencement

1. These Regulations may be cited as the Enduring Powers of Attorney (Prescribed Form) Regulations 1990 and shall come into force on 31st July 1990.

Prescribed form

2.—(1) Subject to paragraphs (2) and (3) of this regulation and to regulation 4, an enduring power of attorney must be in the form set out in the Schedule to these Regulations and must include all the explanatory information headed 'About using this form' in Part A of the Schedule and all the relevant marginal notes to Parts B and C. It may also include such additions (including paragraph numbers) or restrictions as the donor may decide.

(2) In completing the form of enduring power of attorney—
- (a) there shall be excluded (either by omission or deletion)—
  - (i) where the donor appoints only one attorney, everything between the square brackets on the first page of Part B; and
  - (ii) one and only one of any pair of alternatives;
- (b) there may also be so excluded—
  - (i) the words on the second page of Part B 'subject to the following restrictions and conditions', if those words do not apply;
  - (ii) the attestation details for a second witness in Parts B and C if a second witness is not required; and
  - (iii) any marginal notes which correspond with any words excluded under the provisions of this paragraph and the two notes numbered 1 and 2 which appear immediately under the heading to Part C.

(3) The form of execution by the donor or by an attorney may be adapted to provide—

(a) for a case where the donor or an attorney signs by means of a mark; and

(b) for the case (dealt with in regulation 3) where the enduring power of attorney is executed at the direction of the donor or of an attorney; and the form of execution by an attorney may be adapted to provide for execution by a trust corporation.

(4) Subject to paragraphs (1), (2) and (3) of this regulation and to regulation 4, an enduring power of attorney which seeks to exclude any provision contained in these Regulations is not a valid enduring power of attorney.

Execution

3.—(1) An enduring power of attorney in the form set out in the Schedule to these Regulations shall be executed by both the donor and the attorney, although not necessarily at the same time, in the presence of a witness, but not necessarily the same witness, who shall sign the form and give his full name and address.

(2) The donor and an attorney shall not witness the signature of each other nor one attorney the signature of another.

(3) Where an enduring power of attorney is executed at the direction of the donor—

(a) it must be signed in the presence of two witnesses who shall each sign the form and give their full names and addresses; and

(b) a statement that the enduring power of attorney has been executed at the direction of the donor must be inserted in Part B;

(c) it must not be signed by either an attorney or any of the witnesses to the signature of either the donor or an attorney.

(4) Where an enduring power of attorney is executed at the direction of an attorney—

(a) paragraph (3)(a) above applies; and

(b) a statement that the enduring power of attorney has been executed at the direction of the attorney must be inserted in Part C;

(c) it must not be signed by either the donor, an attorney or any of the witnesses to the signature of either the donor or an attorney.

4. Where more than one attorney is appointed and they are to act jointly and severally, then at least one of the attorneys so appointed must execute the instrument for it to take effect as an enduring power of attorney, and only those attorneys who have executed the instrument shall have the functions of an attorney under an enduring power of attorney in the event of the donor's mental incapacity or of the registration of the power, whichever first occurs.

Revocation

5. The Enduring Powers of Attorney (Prescribed Form) Regulations 1987 are hereby revoked, except that—

(a) a power executed in the form prescribed by those Regulations and executed by the donor before 31st July 1991 shall be capable (whether or not seals are affixed to it) of being a valid enduring power of attorney;

(b) regulation 3(3) shall apply to a power executed by the donor before 31st July 1991 under the provisions of those Regulations and the form of enduring power of attorney prescribed by those Regulations may be modified accordingly.

Dated 5th July 1990   *Mackay of Clashfern, C.*

SCHEDULE
ENDURING POWER OF ATTORNEY

[*This form is reproduced in Appendix 3, Forms of Document, pp 196–201.*]

Forms of Document

CONTENTS

E Companies

A POWERS OF ATTORNEY FOR GENERAL USE

1 Statutory general power

THIS GENERAL POWER OF ATTORNEY is made this   day
of   19
by   of
I appoint   of
[*or*   of
and   of
jointly *or* jointly and severally] to be my attorney[s] in accordance with section
10 of the Powers of Attorney Act 1971.

IN WITNESS etc

*   *   *

2 General power: full form

1 THIS POWER OF ATTORNEY is granted on   19
  1 I,   of
appoint   of
[and   of   ]
to be my attorney[s] [jointly] [jointly and severally] for the following purposes:

(*a*) To manage all my land and buildings, and for that purpose to grant
tenancies and licences, accept tenancies, collect rents and other payments,
enforce tenancy and licence terms, comply with statutory obligations,
contract for services and supplies, and pay outgoings

(*b*) To buy, sell, exchange, charge, encumber, or create or accept any
legal or equitable interest in, land of any tenure

(*c*) To buy, sell and exchange stocks, shares, debentures and other forms
of investment dealt with on the International Stock Exchange and to exercise
all my rights as owner of those investments, including appointing proxies to
attend and vote at meetings on my behalf

(*d*) To carry on any business of mine and for that purpose to occupy and
use my business premises, buy and sell stock, give credit, employ staff, comply
with statutory requirements, advertise, and enter into and comply with
obligations for administering the business

(*e*) To sell any of my goods and to buy clothes, accessories, furniture, household goods, motor vehicles and other articles for my use

(*f*) To open in my name one or more bank accounts of any type and to operate them by depositing, withdrawing and transferring money, and authorising payments direct to the accounts of other people

(*g*) To borrow money on my behalf from such persons and on such terms, as to interest, repayment and security on my property, as my attorney decides

(*h*) To mortgage, charge, pledge, create a lien over, deliver as security, or deposit the title deeds of, all or any of my property

(*i*) To make contracts in my name and to execute and deliver in my name and on my behalf any deed affecting my property or interests, whether or not a deed is necessary in the circumstances

(*j*) To take, defend, accept service of, and take steps in any legal or arbitration proceedings on my behalf, including applying for or concurring in the appointment of an arbitrator, and for that purpose to appear and instruct solicitors and counsel in any court, tribunal or arbitration

(*k*) To agree a compromise or settlement of any claim made by or against me, and the terms on which any litigation or arbitration proceedings are to be settled

(*l*) To accept payment of any money due to me and to give receipts on my behalf to discharge the debtors

(*m*) To make a proposal for, effect and maintain any policy of insurance against any risk to which I or my property or estate may be exposed

(*n*) To engage, commission, instruct, direct and discharge any contractor, adviser, broker or agent on my behalf for any purpose, agreeing their terms of engagement and paying them for the services

(*o*) To employ, give instructions and directions to and to discharge any employee to serve me, fixing his terms of employment, paying him and providing agreed benefits to him provided

(*p*) To appoint in writing, with power to revoke any appointment without giving any reason, a substitute to act as my attorney in his stead under this power (but without the substitute having power to appoint a substitute in his turn) without my attorney having any liability for the acts of any substitute

(*q*) Generally to do all acts on my behalf which I may delegate to an attorney and to manage my affairs as fully as I may myself

2 I undertake to ratify all acts done by my attorney under the authority of this power

IN WITNESS etc

3 Power for particular purpose

THIS POWER OF ATTORNEY is granted on   19
I,   of
appoint   of
to be my attorney for the following purposes:
   1 To [*special purpose*]

   2 For that purpose:

      (*a*) To sign or execute in my name and on my behalf any contract, document or deed

      (*b*) To engage or commission any contractor, advisor or agent, agreeing their terms of engagement and paying them for the services

      (*c*) To do anything else reasonably necessary so that the object can be achieved as effectively as if I had done it myself

   And I undertake to ratify whatever my attorney does under the authority or purported authority of this power

IN WITNESS etc

                        *   *   *

4 Enduring power for general use

Part A: About using this form

   1 You may choose one attorney or more than one. If you choose one attorney then you must delete everything between the square brackets on the first page of the form. If you choose more than one, you must decide whether they are to be able to act:
- Jointly (that is, they must all act together and cannot act separately) or
- Jointly and severally (that is, they can all act together but they can also act separately if they wish).
On the first page of the form show what you have decided by crossing out one of the alternatives.
   2 If you give your attorney(s) general power in relation to all your property and affairs, it means that they will be able to deal with your money or property and may be able to sell your house.
   3 If you don't want your attorney(s) to have such wide powers, you can include any restrictions you like. For example, you can include a restriction that your attorney(s) must not act on your behalf until they have reason to believe that you are becoming mentally incapable; or a restriction as to what

your attorney(s) may do. Any restrictions you choose must be written or typed where indicated on the second page of the form.

4 If you are a trustee (and please remember that co-ownership of a home involves trusteeship), you should seek legal advice if you want your attorney(s) to act as trustee on your behalf.

5 Unless you put in a restriction preventing it your attorney(s) will be able to use any of your money or property to make any provision which you yourself might be expected to make for their own needs or the needs of other people. Your attorney(s) will also be able to use your money to make gifts, but only for reasonable amounts in relation to the value of your money and property.

6 Your attorney(s) can recover the out-of-pocket expenses of acting as your attorney(s). If your attorney(s) are professional people, for example solicitors or accountants, they may be able to charge for their professional services as well. You may wish to provide expressly for the remuneration of your attorney(s) (although if they are trustees they may not be allowed to accept it).

7 If your attorney(s) have reason to believe that you have become or are becoming mentally incapable of managing your affairs, your attorney(s) will have to apply to the Court of Protection for registration of this power.

8 Before applying to the Court of Protection for registration of this power, your attorney(s) must give written notice that that is what they are going to do, to you and your nearest relatives as defined in the Enduring Powers of Attorney Act 1985. You or your relatives will be able to object if you or they disagree with registration.

9 This is a simplified explanation of what the Enduring Powers of Attorney Act 1985 and the Rules and Regulations say. If you need more guidance, you or your advisers will need to look at the Act itself and the Rules and Regulations. The Rules are the Court of Protection (Enduring Powers of Attorney) Rules 1986 (Statutory Instrument 1986 No 127). The Regulations are the Enduring Powers of Attorney (Prescribed Form) Regulations 1990 (Statutory Instrument 1990 No 1376).

10 Note to Attorney(s)
After the power has been registered you should notify the Court of Protection if the donor dies or recovers.

11 Note to Donor
Some of these explanatory notes may not apply to the form you are using if it has already been adapted to suit your particular requirements.
You can cancel this power at any time before it has to be registered.

Part B: To be completed by the 'donor' (the person appointing the attorney(s))

Don't sign this form unless you understand what it means
Please read the notes
in the margin which
follow and which are
part of the form itself

Donor's name and address	I of
Donor's date of birth	born on
	appoint
	of
See note 1. If you are appointing only one attorney you should cross out everything between the square brackets. If appointing more than two attorneys please give the additional name(s) on an attached sheet	• [and of
Cross out the one which does not apply (see Note 1 on the front of this form)	• jointly • jointly and severally] to be my attorney(s) for the purpose of the Enduring Powers of Attorney Act 1985
Cross out the one which does not apply (see note 2 on the front of this form). Add any additional powers	• with general authority to act on my behalf • with authority to do the following on my behalf:
If you don't want the attorney(s) to have general power, you must give details here of what authority you are giving the attorney(s)	
	in relation to
Cross out the one which does not apply	• all my property and affairs: • the following property and affairs:
If there are restrictions or conditions, insert them here; if not, cross out these words	• subject to the following restrictions and conditions:

if you wish (see note 3 on the front of this form)

If this form is being signed at your direction:
● the person signing must not be an attorney or any witness (to Parts B or C).

I intend that this power shall continue even if I become mentally incapable

● you must add a statement that this form has been signed at your direction
● a second witness is necessary (please see below)

I have read or have had read to me the notes in Part A which are part of, and explain, this form.

Your signature (or mark)

Signed by me as a deed

and delivered

Date

on

Signature of witness

in the presence of

Your attorney(s) cannot be your witness. It is not advisable for your husband or wife to be your witness

Full name of witness

Address of witness

A second witness is only necessary if this form is not being signed by you personally but at your direction (for example, if a physical disability prevents you from signing).
Signature of second witness

in the presence of

Full name of witness

Address of witness

Part C: To be completed by the attorney(s)

Note: 1   This form may be adapted to provide for execution by a corporation

Note: 2   If there is more than one attorney additional sheets in the form as shown below must be added to this Part C

Please read the notes in the margin which follow and which are part of the form itself

Don't sign this form before the donor has signed Part B or if, in your opinion, the donor was already mentally incapable at the time of signing Part B

I understand that I have a duty to apply to the Court for the registration of this form under the Enduring Powers of Attorney Act 1985 when the donor is becoming or has become mentally incapable.

I also understand my limited power to use the donor's property to benefit persons other than the donor.

If this form is being signed at your direction:
● the person signing must not be an attorney or any witness (to Parts B or C)
● you must add a statement that this form has been signed at your direction
● a second witness is necessary (please see below)

I am not a minor

Signature (or mark) of attorney.

Signed by me as a deed

and delivered

Date

on

Signature of witness

in the presence of

The attorney must sign the form and his signature must be witnessed. The donor may not be the witness and one attorney may not

Full name of witness

Address of witness

witness the signature
of the other

A second witness is
only necessary if this
form is not being
signed by you
personally but at
your direction (for
example, if a physical
disability prevents
you from signing)

Signature of second
witness

in the presence of

Full name of witness

Address of witness

*   *   *

5 Enduring power for spouse to sell matrimonial home

Part A: About using this form

1 You may choose one attorney or more than one. If you choose one attorney then you must delete everything between the square brackets on the first page of the form. If you choose more than one, you must decide whether they are to be able to act:
- Jointly (that is, they must all act together and cannot act separately) or
- Jointly and severally (that is, they can all act together but they can also act separately if they wish).

On the first page of the form show what you have decided by crossing out one of the alternatives.

2 If you give your attorney(s) general power in relation to all your property and affairs, it means that they will be able to deal with your money or property and may be able to sell your house.

3 If you don't want your attorney(s) to have such wide powers, you can include any restrictions you like. For example, you can include a restriction that your attorney(s) must not act on your behalf until they have reason to believe that you are becoming mentally incapable; or a restriction as to what your attorney(s) may do. Any restrictions you choose must be written or typed where indicated on the second page of the form.

4 If you are a trustee (and please remember that co-ownership of a home involves trusteeship), you should seek legal advice if you want your attorney(s) to act as trustee on your behalf.

5 Unless you put in a restriction preventing it your attorney(s) will be able to use any of your money or property to make any provision which you yourself might be expected to make for their own needs or the needs of other people. Your attorney(s) will also be able to use your money to make gifts, but only for reasonable amounts in relation to the value of your money and property.

6 Your attorney(s) can recover the out-of-pocket expenses of acting as your attorney(s). If your attorney(s) are professional people, for example solicitors or accountants, they may be able to charge for their professional services as well. You may wish to provide expressly for the remuneration of your attorney(s) (although if they are trustees they may not be allowed to accept it).

7 If your attorney(s) have reason to believe that you have become or are becoming mentally incapable of managing your affairs, your attorney(s) will have to apply to the Court of Protection for registration of this power.

8 Before applying to the Court of Protection for registration of this power, your attorney(s) must give written notice that that is what they are going to do, to you and your nearest relatives as defined in the Enduring Powers of Attorney Act 1985. You or your relatives will be able to object if you or they disagree with registration.

9 This is a simplified explanation of what the Enduring Powers of Attorney Act 1985 and the Rules and Regulations say. If you need more guidance, you or your advisers will need to look at the Act itself and the Rules and Regulations. The Rules are the Court of Protection (Enduring Powers of Attorney) Rules 1986 (Statutory Instrument 1986 No 127). The Regulations are the Enduring Powers of Attorney (Prescribed Form) Regulations 1990 (Statutory Instrument 1990 No 1376).

10 Note to Attorney(s)
After the power has been registered you should notify the Court of Protection if the donor dies or recovers.

11 Note to Donor
Some of these explanatory notes may not apply to the form you are using if it has already been adapted to suit your particular requirements.
You can cancel this power at any time before it has to be registered.

Part B: To be completed by the 'donor' (the person appointing the attorney(s))

Don't sign this form unless you understand what it means
Please read the notes
in the margin which
follow and which are
part of the form itself

Donor's name and address	I of
Donor's date of birth	born on
	appoint my [wife] [husband]
	of

to be my attorney for the purpose of the Enduring Powers of Attorney Act 1985 with authority to do the following on my behalf:

If you don't want the attorney(s) to have general power, you must give details here of what authority you are giving the attorney(s)

(1) To sell, lease or otherwise dispose of my legal and equitable interests

(2) To apply the proceeds of any disposition in the discharge of the subsisting mortgage debt and in settling any outgoings or liabilities

(3) To instruct agents and professional advisers for these purposes

(4) To execute deeds, sign contracts and do or authorise all other acts which my attorney considers necessary for these purposes in relation to the following property and affairs:
our property, 'Blackacre', Casterbridge [registered at H M Land Registry under Title Number   ]

If there are restrictions or conditions, insert them here; if not, cross out these words if you wish (see note 3 on the front of this form)

● subject to the following restrictions and conditions:

(a) My attorney has no power to exercise any trust, power or discretion which I have as trustee other than in relation to that property

(b) My attorney has no power to benefit or make gifts to any person on my behalf, nor to dispose of, deal with, manage, meddle with or in any way affect anything I own other than that property any interest in it

[(c) This power ceases to have effect at the end of two years from the date I signed it]

If this form is being signed at your direction:
● the person signing must not be an attorney or any witness (to Parts B or C)
● you must add a statement that this form has been signed at your direction
● a second witness is necessary (please see below)

I intend that this power shall continue even if I become mentally incapable

I have read or have had read to me the notes in Part A which are part of, and explain, this form.

Your signature (or mark)

Signed by me as a deed

and delivered

Date

on

Signature of witness

in the presence of

Your attorney(s) cannot be your witness. It is not advisable for your husband or wife to be your witness

Full name of witness

Address of witness

A second witness is only necessary if this form is not being signed by you personally but at your direction (for example, if a physical disability prevents you from signing) Signature of second witness

in the presence of

Full name of witness

Address of witness

Part C: *To be completed by the attorney(s)*

Please read the notes in the margin which follow and which are part of the form itself

Don't sign this form before the donor has signed Part B or if, in your opinion, the donor was already mentally incapable at the time of signing Part B

I understand that I have a duty to apply to the Court for the registration of this form under the Enduring Powers of Attorney Act 1985 when the donor is becoming or has become mentally incapable.

I also understand my limited power to use the donor's property to benefit persons other than the donor.

If this form is being signed at your direction:
● the person signing must not be an attorney or any

I am not a minor

witness (to Parts B or
C)
● you must add a
statement that this
form has been signed
at your direction
● a second witness is
necessary (please see
below)

Signature (or mark)
of attorney.

Signed by me as a deed
and delivered

Date

on

Signature of witness

in the presence of

The attorney must
sign the form and his
signature must be
witnessed. The donor
may not be the
witness and one
attorney may not
witness the signature
of the other

Full name of witness

Address of witness

A second witness is
only necessary if this
form is not being
signed by you
personally but at
your direction (for
example, if a physical
disability prevents
you from signing)

Signature of second
witness

in the presence of

Full name of witness

Address of witness

B ANCILLARY DOCUMENTS

6 Appointment of substitute

1 I   of
was appointed attorney by   of

('the Donor') by a Power of Attorney dated   19   ('the Power of Attorney')

2 The Power of Attorney gave me authority to appoint a substitute to act as attorney instead of me as if he had originally been appointed by the Power of Attorney

3 I appoint   of
to be my substitute and act as attorney of the Donor under the Power of Attorney

4 This appointment is subject to the right given to me by the Power of Attorney to revoke any appointments as I think fit

Date: 19
Signed:

*   *   *

7 Revocation of appointment of substitute

1 I   of
was appointed attorney by   of
('the Donor') by a Power of Attorney dated   19   ('the Power of Attorney')

2 On   19   I appointed   of
('the substitute') to be my substitute as attorney of the Grantor

3 The Power of Attorney gave me authority to revoke any appointment of a substitute

4 I revoke the appointment of the substitute as attorney under the Power of Attorney

Date: 19
Signed

*   *   *

8 Deed of disclaimer

1 I   of   was appointed attorney
[together with   of   ]
by   of   ('the Donor') by a Power of Attorney dated dated   19   ('the Power of Attorney')

2 I disclaim the authority conferred on me by the Power of Attorney so that I shall not be capable or entitled to exercise or to join in exercising it

[3 This deed does affect the authority conferred by the Power of Attorney on anyone other than me]

IN WITNESS etc

* * *

9 Deed of revocation

THIS DEED OF REVOCATION is made on the   day of   19
by   of

1 I granted a Power of Attorney dated   19   ('the Power of Attorney') appointing   of   [together with   of   to act] [jointly] [jointly and severally] to be my attorney[s]

2 I revoke the Power of Attorney and the authority granted by it

3 This deed is not to prejudice my undertaking in the Power of Attorney to ratify the acts already done by my attorney[s] under it

IN WITNESS etc

* * *

10 Statutory declaration of nonrevocation: ordinary power

[I] [We]
of
solemnly and sincerely [jointly] declare:

On   19   [I] [we] dealt with
who [was] [were] appointed attorney[s] by a Power of Attorney dated   19   granted by

[I was] [we were] not then aware that the power had been revoked

[I [WE] make this solemn declaration conscientiously believing the same to be true and by virtue of the Statutory Declarations Act 1835

Declared etc

* * *

11 Statutory declaration of nonrevocation: enduring power

[I] [WE]
of
solemnly and sincerely [jointly] declare:

1 On   19   [I] [we] dealt with
who [was] [were] appointed attorney[s] by a Power of Attorney dated
        19   granted by

2 [I] [WE] had then no reason to doubt that the attorney[s] had power to dispose of the property which was the subject of that transaction

[I] [WE] make this solemn declaration conscientiously believing the same to be true and by virtue of the Statutory Declarations Act 1835

Declared etc

*   *   *

12 Statutory declaration of nonrevocation: ordinary power, for land registration purposes

[I] [WE]
of
solemnly and sincerely [jointly] declare:

1 On   19   [I] [we] completed a transaction with
who [was] [were] appointed attorney[s] by a Power of Attorney
dated   19   ('the Power') granted by   ('the donor').

2 [I] [we] did not then know of
   (*a*) any revocation of the Power, or

   (*b*) the occurrence of any event (such as death, bankruptcy or other incapacity of the donor) which had the effect of revoking the Power

[I] [WE] make this solemn declaration conscientiously believing the same to be true and by virtue of the Statutory Declarations Act 1835

Declared etc

*   *   *

13 Statutory declaration of nonrevocation: enduring power, for land registration purposes

[I] [WE]
of
solemnly and sincerely [jointly] declare:

1 ON   19   [I] [we] completed a transaction with
who [was] [were] appointed attorney[s] by a Power of Attorney
dated   19   ('the Power') granted by   ('the donor').

2 [I] [we] did not then know of

(*a*) any revocation of the Power whether by the donor or by the Court of Protection, or

(*b*) of the occurrence of any event (such as death or bankruptcy of the donor, the bankruptcy of the attorney [or [any] [either] of them] or a direction by the Court of Protection on exercising its powers under Part VII of the Mental Health Act 1983) which had the effect of revoking the Power, or

(*c*) that the Power was not a valid enduring power of attorney and had been revoked by the donor's mental incapacity

[I] [WE] make this solemn declaration conscientiously believing the same to be true and by virtue of the Statutory Declarations Act 1835

Declared etc

*   *   *

C TRUSTEES

14 Ordinary power of attorney granted by trustee

BY THIS POWER OF ATTORNEY dated   19
I,
appoint ('my attorney')
in accordance with section 25 of the Trustee Act 1925, as amended, as my attorney, in my name and on my behalf:

1 To act for the period of   from   19
as trustee of
jointly with the other trustee(s) for the time being, executing and exercising the trusts, powers and discretions that I have in that capacity both under the trust instrument and by statute

2 For that purpose to sign or execute any document or deed

I undertake to ratify whatever my attorney does under the authority or the purported authority of this power

IN WITNESS etc

*   *   *

15 Enduring power of attorney granted by trustee: all trusts

Part A: About using this form

1 **You may choose one attorney or more than one.** If you choose one attorney then you must delete everything between the square brackets on the

first page of the form. If you choose more than one, you must decide whether they are to be able to act:

- Jointly (that is, they must all act together and cannot act separately) or
- Jointly and severally (that is, they can all act together but they can also act separately if they wish).

On the first page of the form show what you have decided by crossing out one of the alternatives.

2 If you give your attorney(s) general power in relation to all your property and affairs, it means that they will be able to deal with your money or property and may be able to sell your house.

3 If you don't want your attorney(s) to have such wide powers, you can include any restrictions you like. For example, you can include a restriction that your attorney(s) must not act on your behalf until they have reason to believe that you are becoming mentally incapable; or a restriction as to what your attorney(s) may do. Any restrictions you choose must be written or typed where indicated on the second page of the form.

4 If you are a trustee (and please remember that co-ownership of a home involves trusteeship), you should seek legal advice if you want your attorney(s) to act as trustee on your behalf.

5 Unless you put in a restriction preventing it your attorney(s) will be able to use any of your money or property to make any provision which you yourself might be expected to make for their own needs or the needs of other people. Your attorney(s) will also be able to use your money to make gifts, but only for reasonable amounts in relation to the value of your money and property.

6 Your attorney(s) can recover the out-of-pocket expenses of acting as your attorney(s). If your attorney(s) are professional people, for example solicitors or accountants, they may be able to charge for their professional services as well. You may wish to provide expressly for the remuneration of your attorney(s) (although if they are trustees they may not be allowed to accept it).

7 If your attorney(s) have reason to believe that you have become or are becoming mentally incapable of managing your affairs, your attorney(s) will have to apply to the Court of Protection for registration of this power.

8 Before applying to the Court of Protection for registration of this power, your attorney(s) must give written notice that that is what they are going to do, to you and your nearest relatives as defined in the Enduring Powers of Attorney Act 1985. You or your relatives will be able to object if you or they disagree with registration.

9 This is a simplified explanation of what the Enduring Powers of Attorney Act 1985 and the Rules and Regulations say. If you need more guidance, you or your advisers will need to look at the Act itself and the Rules and Regulations. The Rules are the Court of Protection (Enduring Powers of Attorney) Rules 1986 (Statutory Instrument 1986 No 127). The Regulations are the Enduring Powers of Attorney (Prescribed Form) Regulations 1990 (Statutory Instrument 1990 No 1376).

10 Note to Attorney(s)

After the power has been registered you should notify the Court of Protection if the donor dies or recovers.

11 Note to Donor

Some of these explanatory notes may not apply to the form you are using if it has already been adapted to suit your particular requirements.
You can cancel this power at any time before it has to be registered.

Part B: To be completed by the 'donor' (the person appointing the attorney(s))

Don't sign this form unless you understand what it means
Please read the notes
in the margin which
follow and which are
part of the form itself

Donor's name and address	I of
Donor's date of birth	born on
	appoint
	of

to be my attorney for the purpose of the Enduring Powers of Attorney Act 1985 with authority to do the following on my behalf:

If you don't want the attorney(s) to have general power, you must give details here of what authority you are giving the attorney(s)

To exercise all the trust, powers and discretions which I have as trustee of all the trusts, settlements and estates of which I have been appointed trustee, in each case jointly with the respective other trustees in relation to the following property and affairs:
all the assets for the time being respectively belonging to the trust, settlement or estate in question

If this form is being signed at your direction:
● the person signing must not be an attorney or any witness (to Parts B or C)

I intend that this power shall continue even if I become mentally incapable

● you must add a statement that this form has been signed at your direction
● a second witness is

I have read or have had read to me the notes in Part A which are part of, and explain, this form.

necessary (please see below)

Your signature (or mark)	Signed by me as a deed and delivered
Date	on
Signature of witness	in the presence of

Your attorney(s) cannot be your witness. It is not advisable for your husband or wife to be your witness

Full name of witness

Address of witness

A second witness is only necessary if this form is not being signed by you personally but at your direction (for example, if a physical disability prevents you from signing)

Signature of second witness

in the presence of

Full name of witness

Address of witness

Part C: To be completed by the attorney(s)

Please read the notes in the margin which follow and which are part of the form itself

Don't sign this form before the donor has signed Part B or if, in your opinion, the donor was already mentally incapable at the time of signing Part B

I understand that I have a duty to apply to the Court for the registration of this form under the Enduring Powers of Attorney Act 1985 when the donor is becoming or has become mentally incapable.

I also understand my limited power to use the donor's property to benefit persons other than the donor.

If this form is being signed at your direction:

I am not a minor

- the person signing must not be an attorney or any witness (to Parts B or C)
- you must add a statement that this form has been signed at your direction
- a second witness is necessary (please see below)

Signature (or mark) of attorney.

Signed by me as a deed and delivered

Date

on

Signature of witness

in the presence of

The attorney must sign the form and his signature must be witnessed. The donor may not be the witness and one attorney may not witness the signature of the other

Full name of witness

Address of witness

A second witness is only necessary if this form is not being signed by you personally but at your direction (for example, if a physical disability prevents you from signing)

Signature of second witness

in the presence of

Full name of witness

Address of witness

*   *   *

16 Enduring power of attorney granted by trustee: one trust

Part A: About using this form

1 You may choose one attorney or more than one. If you choose one attorney then you must delete everything between the square brackets on the first page of the form. If you choose more than one, you must decide whether they are to be able to act:

- Jointly (that is, they must all act together and cannot act separately) or
- Jointly and severally (that is, they can all act together but they can also act separately if they wish).

On the first page of the form show what you have decided by crossing out one of the alternatives.

2 If you give your attorney(s) general power in relation to all your property and affairs, it means that they will be able to deal with your money or property and may be able to sell your house.

3 If you don't want your attorney(s) to have such wide powers, you can include any restrictions you like. For example, you can include a restriction that your attorney(s) must not act on your behalf until they have reason to believe that you are becoming mentally incapable; or a restriction as to what your attorney(s) may do. Any restrictions you choose must be written or typed where indicated on the second page of the form.

4 If you are a trustee (and please remember that co-ownership of a home involves trusteeship), you should seek legal advice if you want your attorney(s) to act as trustee on your behalf.

5 Unless you put in a restriction preventing it your attorney(s) will be able to use any of your money or property to make any provision which you yourself might be expected to make for their own needs or the needs of other people. Your attorney(s) will also be able to use your money to make gifts, but only for reasonable amounts in relation to the value of your money and property.

6 Your attorney(s) can recover the out-of-pocket expenses of acting as your attorney(s). If your attorney(s) are professional people, for example solicitors or accountants, they may be able to charge for their professional services as well. You may wish to provide expressly for the remuneration of your attorney(s) (although if they are trustees they may not be allowed to accept it).

7 If your attorney(s) have reason to believe that you have become or are becoming mentally incapable of managing your affairs, your attorney(s) will have to apply to the Court of Protection for registration of this power.

8 Before applying to the Court of Protection for registration of this power, your attorney(s) must give written notice that that is what they are going to do, to you and your nearest relatives as defined in the Enduring Powers of Attorney Act 1985. You or your relatives will be able to object if you or they disagree with registration.

9 This is a simplified explanation of what the Enduring Powers of Attorney Act 1985 and the Rules and Regulations say. If you need more guidance, you or your advisers will need to look at the Act itself and the Rules and Regulations. The Rules are the Court of Protection (Enduring Powers of

Attorney) Rules 1986 (Statutory Instrument 1986 No 127). The Regulations are the Enduring Powers of Attorney (Prescribed Form) Regulations 1990 (Statutory Instrument 1990 No 1376).

10 Note to Attorney(s)

After the power has been registered you should notify the Court of Protection if the donor dies or recovers.

11 Note to Donor

Some of these explanatory notes may not apply to the form you are using if it has already been adapted to suit your particular requirements.

You can cancel this power at any time before it has to be registered.

Part B: To be completed by the 'donor' (the person appointing the attorney(s))

Don't sign this form unless you understand what it means
Please read the notes
in the margin which
follow and which are
part of the form itself

Donor's name and address	I of
Donor's date of birth	born on
	appoint
	of
	to be my attorney for the purpose of the Enduring Powers of Attorney Act 1985 with authority to do the following on my behalf:
If you don't want the general power, you must give details here of what authority you are giving the attorney(s)	To exercise all my trusts, powers and discretions as trustee of . . . ('the Trust') jointly with the other trustees of the Trust in relation to the following property and affairs: all the assets for the time being of the Trust
If this form is being signed at your direction:	I intend that this power shall continue even if I become mentally incapable
● the person signing must not be an attorney or any witness (to Parts B or C)	
● you must add a statement that this	I have read or have had read to me the notes in Part A which are part of, and explain, this form.

form has been signed
at your direction
● a second witness is
necessary (please see
below)

Your signature (or
mark)

Signed by me as a deed

and delivered

Date

on

Signature of witness

in the presence of

Your attorney(s)
cannot be your
witness. It is not
advisable for your
husband or wife to
be your witness

Full name of witness

Address of witness

A second witness is
only necessary if this
form is not being
signed by you
personally but at
your direction (for
example, if a physical
disability prevents
you from signing)
Signature of second
witness

in the presence of

Full name of witness

Address of witness

Part C: To be completed by the attorney(s)

Please read the notes
in the margin which
follow and which are
part of the form itself

Don't sign this form
before the donor has
signed Part B or if, in
your opinion, the
donor was already
mentally incapable at
the time of signing
Part B

I understand that I have a duty to apply to the
Court for the registration of this form under the
Enduring Powers of Attorney Act 1985 when the
donor is becoming or has become mentally
incapable.

I also understand my limited power to use the
donor's property to benefit persons other than
the donor.

If this form is being signed at your direction:
● the person signing must not be an attorney or any witness (to Parts B or C)
● you must add a statement that this form has been signed at your direction
● a second witness is necessary (please see below)

I am not a minor

Signature (or mark) of attorney.

Signed by me as a deed

and delivered

Date

on

Signature of witness

in the presence of

The attorney must sign the form and his signature must be witnessed. The donor may not be the witness and one attorney may not witness the signature of the other

Full name of witness

Address of witness

A second witness is only necessary if this form is not being signed by you personally but at your direction (for example, if a physical disability prevents you from signing)

Signature of second witness

in the presence of

Full name of witness

Address of witness

*   *   *

17 Power of attorney granted by trustees as a body

THIS POWER OF ATTORNEY is granted on   19

WE,   of
and   of
as the present trustees of   ('the Trust')
appoint   of
to be our attorney for any of the following purposes in relation to the
property of the Trust which is for the time being [outside the United
Kingdom] [in   ]:

To manage, administer or sell all or any of it for that purpose:

(*a*) To sign or execute in our name and on our behalf any contract,
document or deed

(*b*) To engage or commission any contractor, advisor or agent, agreeing
their terms of engagement and paying them for the services

2 This power gives the attorney no authority in relation to:

(*a*) any property of the trust [within the United Kingdom] [beyond the
geographic limits specified above]

(*b*) Any property belonging to us or to any of us either beneficially or in
any capacity other than as trustee of the Trust

And we undertake to ratify whatever our attorney does under the authority
or purported authority of this power

IN WITNESS etc

*   *   *

18 Notice of grant of power

To
I have, by power of attorney, delegated all my trusts, powers and discretions
as trustee of
to   of

The power comes into operation on   and lasts for
              . It was granted because

Date:

Signed:

Name and address:

*   *   *

D PERSONAL REPRESENTATIVES

19 Power of attorney granted by executor

IN THE HIGH COURT OF JUSTICE
Family Division
The [Principal] [District Probate] Registry [at   ]
THIS POWER OF ATTORNEY is granted on   19
by   of
   1   late of   deceased ('the Deceased')
died on   19   having executed his last will dated   19
[and codicil dated   ] which appointed me his executor [executrix]
[together with   as co-executors]

   2 I appoint   of   to be my attorney for
the purpose of obtaining letters of administration of the estate of the
Deceased to be granted to him for my use and benefit and until further
representation be granted

   3 I undertake to ratify whatever my attorney does or causes to be done
under the authority of this power

IN WITNESS etc

*   *   *

20 Power of attorney granted by person entitled to be administrator

IN THE HIGH COURT OF JUSTICE
Family Division
The [Principal] [District Probate] Registry [at   ]
THIS POWER OF ATTORNEY is granted on   19
by   of
   1   late of   deceased ('the Deceased')
died on   19   intestate leaving

   2 I am the lawful   of the Deceased

   3 I appoint   of   to be my attorney for
the purpose of obtaining letters of administration of the estate of the
Deceased to be granted to him for my use and benefit and until further
representation be granted

   4 I undertake to ratify whatever my attorney does or causes to be done
under the authority of this power

IN WITNESS etc

*   *   *

E COMPANIES

21 General proxy

I   of
a member of   [Limited] [plc] ('the Company')
appoint   of   as my proxy to do the
following on my behalf:

(a) To attend, [speak] and vote at meetings of all or any class of
shareholders of the Company which I would be entitled to attend

(b) To requisition or join in requisitioning any meeting

(c) To appoint a substitute to act as my proxy instead of him

Dated:

Signed:

IN WITNESS etc

*   *   *

22 General proxy for one meeting

I   of
a member of   [Limited] [plc] ('the Company'), appoint as
my proxy to attend, [speak] and vote for me at the [Annual] [Extraordinary]
General Meeting of the Company to be held on   19   and at any
adjournment of it:
                  of   , or failing him
of   , or failing him the Chairman of the meeting

Dated:

Signed:

*   *   *

23 Special proxy

I   of
a member of   [Limited] [plc] ('the Company'), appoint as
my proxy on my behalf to attend, [speak] and vote in accordance with the
instructions below at the [Annual] [Extraordinary] General Meeting of the
Company to be held on   19   and at any adjournment of it:
                  of   , or failing him
of   or
failing him the Chairman of the meeting

My proxy is to vote
For/Against* Resolution No 1 on the Notice convening the meeting
For/Against* Resolution No 2 on the Notice convening the meeting
etc

Dated:

Signed:

* Delete one alternative

* * *

24 Directors' resolution appointing the representative

Company shareholder

IT IS RESOLVED that   be the representative of the
Company to attend any meetings of   [Limited] [plc] or of
a class of members of that company to exercise the rights of the Company as a
shareholder in it

Company creditor

IT IS RESOLVED that   be the representative of the
Company to attend any meeting of the creditors of
[Limited] [plc] to exercise the rights of the Company as creditor of it

* * *

25 Statutory declaration of nonrevocation: for Stock Exchange purposes
[I] [WE]
of
solemnly and sincerely [jointly] declare:

1 [I was] [We were] appointed attorney[s] by a Power of Attorney ('the
Power') dated   19   granted by

2 On   19   [I] [we] executed the following transfer[s] for the
purposes of [a] stock exchange transaction[s]:
Security: Transferee[s]:
and on that date the Power had not been revoked.

[I] [WE] make this solemn declaration conscientiously believing the same to
be true and by virtue of the Statutory Declarations Act 1835

Declared etc

* * *

Clauses for Powers of Attorney

A Appointment

Firm as attorney	I appoint the partners for the time being in the firm of ABC & Co solicitors jointly and severally to be my attorneys. This power shall at any time have effect as if it had individually named the then partners in that firm
Nominated partner as attorney	I appoint as my attorney the partner in the firm of ABC & Co solicitors nominated by the firm's then senior partner. No change in the constitution of the firm shall affect the appointment of my attorney, but the then senior partner may at any time revoke a nomination and make another
Company nominee as attorney	I appoint as my attorney the director or employee of XYZ Ltd nominated by resolution of the board of directors of the company. The board may at any time revoke a nomination and make another
One attorney until child attains 21, then eldest child	I appoint as my attorney (*a*) AB, for the period until one of my children attains the age of 21 years (*b*) the first of my children to attain the age of 21 years, for the period beginning when he or she attains that age
Trustee in bankruptcy	I, as the trustee of the estate of AB, a bankrupt, appoint CD of to be my attorney

B Authority conferred on attorney

To manage property	To manage [all my houses and flats] [my house 'Blackacre', Casterbridge,] and for that purpose to grant tenancies and licences, accept tenancies and surrenders of them, collect rents and other payments, enforce tenancy and licence terms, take defend and compromise legal and arbitration

proceedings, comply with statutory obligations, contract for services and supplies, pay outgoings and employ agents and professional advisers

To sell house
To sell my house 'Blackacre', Casterbridge, by private treaty or public auction for at least £   [gross] [after deduction of sale expenses] and for that purpose to sign and execute all necessary documents and deeds and employ agents and professional advisers

To buy house
To buy ['Blackacre', Casterbridge,] [a house for me to occupy with my family] for no more than £   [including] [excluding] purchase expenses and for that purpose to sign and execute all necessary documents and deeds and employ agents and professional advisers

To take lease
To take a lease or tenancy agreement of living accommodation for my family on such terms and conditions as he thinks fit

To deal in land
To buy, sell, exchange, charge, encumber, or create or accept any legal or equitable interest in, land of any tenure and for that purpose to sign and execute all necessary documents and deeds and to employ agents and professional advisers

To manage investments
To buy, sell and exchange stocks, shares, debentures and other forms of investment dealt with on the International Stock Exchange and to exercise all my rights as owner of those investments, including appointing proxies to attend and vote at meetings on my behalf, and for those purposes to sign all necessary documents and employ agents and professional advisers

To consult a stock-broker
To consult a member of the International Stock Exchange before acquiring any investment for me or dealing with any of my investments. No person dealing with my attorney shall be concerned to ensure that he has consulted as required

To carry on business
To carry on my business of   at   and for that purpose to occupy and use my business premises, buy and sell stock, give credit, employ staff, comply with statutory requirements, advertise, and enter into and comply with obligations for administering the business

To sell chattels
To sell [my motor car number   ] [all my goods in England] for [a total of] [not less than

£   ] [what he thinks fit] and to pay the net proceeds into my bank account with   Bank plc, Casterbridge, and for that purpose to advertise and employ agents

To operate bank accounts	To open in my name one or more accounts of any type with Bank plc, Casterbridge, and to operate them by depositing, withdrawing and transferring money, and authorising payments direct to the accounts of other people [but without power to borrow money from the bank for me]
To borrow money	To borrow money on my behalf [for the purposes mentioned above] from such persons and on such terms, as to interest, repayment and security on my property, as my attorney decides
To mortgage	To mortgage, charge, pledge, create a lien over, deliver as security, or deposit the title deeds of, all or any of my property
To execute deeds	To execute and deliver in my name and on my behalf any deed affecting my property or interests, whether or not a deed is necessary in the circumstances
To litigate	To take, defend, accept service of, and take steps in any legal proceedings on my behalf and for that purpose to appear and instruct solicitors and counsel in any court or tribunal
To arbitrate	To seek a settlement of any dispute to which I am a party by agreeing to arbitrate, concurring in the appointment of an arbitrator or the reference of the dispute to one, to take or defend arbitration proceedings and to instruct solicitors and counsel for that purpose
To compromise claims	To agree a compromise or settlement of any claim made by or against me, and the terms on which any litigation or arbitration proceedings are to be settled
To give receipts	To accept payment of any money due to me and to give receipts on my behalf to discharge the debtors
To insure	To make a proposal for, effect and maintain any policy of insurance against any risk to which I or my property or estate may be exposed
To employ independent contractors	To engage, commission, instruct, direct and discharge any contractor, adviser or agent on my behalf for any purpose, agreeing their terms of engagement and paying them for the services

| To employ servants | To employ, give instructions and directions to and to discharge any employee to serve me, fixing his terms of employment, paying him and providing agreed benefits to him |
| To charge fees | To charge professional fees for all work done in exercising the authority which I am granting to my attorney by this power, and to pay himself the amount of those fees from any money belonging to me |

C Restrictions on authority

Not to exercise trustee powers	This power of attorney does not give [any of] my attorney[s] power to execute or exercise any trust, power or discretion which I have as trustee
Not to benefit or make gifts to attorney[s]	This power of attorney does not give [any of] my attorney[s] power to benefit or make gifts to [himself] [herself] [themselves or any of them] from my property
Not to make gifts to charity	This power of attorney does not give [any of] my attorney[s] power to make gifts to charity from my property
Only to benefit or make gifts to relatives	The only people whom my attorney[s] may benefit or make gifts to from my estate are my [wife] [husband] and my relatives of the whole blood
Limit on value of gifts and benefits	In any one calendar year, my attorney[s] shall not make gifts or confer gratuitous benefits from my estate totalling more than [£5,000] [five per cent of the then total value of my property]
Spouse's agreement to house sale	Only to sell or mortgage my house 'Blackacre', Casterbridge, with the written concurrence of my [wife] [husband]
Delay acting until receipt of confirmation	My attorney shall not exercise the authority this power confers on him until he receives a confirmatory letter signed by me [and witnessed by a consular officer] and attaches the letter to this deed

D Manner of exercising powers

| Act in donor's name | My attorney is to act and sign in my name and expressly on my behalf when executing any deed, signing any contract or doing any other act under his authority as my attorney |
| Power to appoint substitutes | My attorney may at any time appoint a substitute to act as my attorney, and may revoke any |

appointment without giving a reason. Every appointment is to be in writing signed by my attorney. Every substitute has full powers as my attorney, as if appointed by this deed, except this power to appoint a substitute

Limited substitute

My attorney may at any time appoint as a substitute a partner in his solicitor's firm to act as my attorney, and may revoke an appointment at any time. Every appointment is to be in writing signed by my attorney. Every substitute has full power as my attorney, as if appointed by this deed, except this power to appoint a substitute. No one dealing with a substitute shall be concerned to enquire whether he is qualified for appointment

Corporate attorney's representative

My attorney may at any time by resolution of its board of directors appoint one of its officers to exercise the authority of my attorney in his name but on its behalf, and may by a similar resolution revoke any appointment. Anyone dealing with a person purporting to be appointed by resolution may accept a copy of the resolution certified as a true copy by the secretary of the company as conclusive proof of the appointment

E General

Ratification

I agree to ratify all acts done, deeds executed and contracts signed by my attorney on my behalf under the authority or purported authority of this power

Irrevocability

This power is given by way of security to secure [a proprietary interest of my attorney] [the performance of an obligation owed to my attorney] and I declare that this deed is irrevocable

Power irrevocable for fixed period

As part of the bargain with my attorney I agreed to grant the authority conferred by this power for the period of [ten years] from the date of this deed. This power of attorney is irrevocable for that period

F Execution

Person unable to read

SIGNED AS A DEED AND DELIVERED by [the donor], after [I] [someone in my presence] had read and explained to [him] [her] the terms of the deed and [s]he stated that [s]he understood, in the presence of:

Person unable to read: enduring power

SIGNED AS A DEED AND DELIVERED by [the donor], and [I] [someone in my presence] read and explained to [him] [her] the terms of the deed and the explanatory notes forming part of it and [s]he stated that [s]he understood and appeared to appreciate the nature and meaning of it, in the presence of:

Person unable to write or physically disabled

SIGNED AS A DEED AND DELIVERED by AB by direction and in the presence of [the donor] and in the presence also of:

[Two witnesses]

Index